PHILIP WHITEHEAD

DEMONISING THE OTHER

The criminalisation of morality

POLICY PRESS SHORTS RESEARCH

First published in Great Britain in 2018 by

Policy Press
University of Bristol
1-9 Old Park Hill
Bristol
BS2 8BB
UK
t: +44 (0)117 954 5940
pp-info@bristol.ac.uk
www.policypress.co.uk

North America office:
Policy Press
c/o The University of Chicago Press
1427 East 60th Street
Chicago, IL 60637, USA
t: +1 773 702 7700
f: +1 773 702 9756
sales@press.uchicago.edu
www.press.uchicago.edu

© Policy Press 2018

British Library Cataloguing in Publication Data
A catalogue record for this book is available from the British Library.

Library of Congress Cataloging-in-Publication Data
A catalog record for this book has been requested.

ISBN 978-1-4473-4341-7 (hardback)
ISBN 978-1-4473-4343-1 (ePub)
ISBN 978-1-4473-4344-8 (Mobi)
ISBN 978-1-4473-4342-4 (ePDF)

The right of Philip Whitehead to be identified as the author of this work has been asserted by him in accordance with the Copyright, Designs and Patents Act 1988.

The statements and opinions contained within this publication are solely those of the author and not of the University of Bristol or Policy Press. The University of Bristol and Policy Press disclaim responsibility for any injury to persons or property resulting from any material published in this publication.

Policy Press works to counter discrimination on grounds of gender, race, disability, age and sexuality.

Cover design by Policy Press
Front cover: image kindly supplied by istock
Printed and bound in Great Britain by CPI Group (UK) Ltd, Croydon, CR0 4YY
Policy Press uses environmentally responsible print partners

Desire, at the end, was a malady, or a madness, or both. I grew careless of the lives of others. I took pleasure where it pleased me, and passed on.

(Oscar Wilde, 1986, p 152)

I have always believed that it is only in association with others that one finds oneself – and, for an artist, contact with other artists is absolutely necessary for the growth of his personality.

(Peter Ackroyd, 1983, p 64)

In this context the unquestioned hegemony of the market is accompanied by the exhibition of a penal power against the new enemies of the existing order.

(De Giorgi, 2006, p 118)

Human existence is primordially a matter of mutual recognition, and it is only through mutual recognition that we are self-aware and strive for the social meanings in our lives.

(Solomon, 1988, p 68)

Contents

Prologue

The ethical question confronting all of us without exception, and with a pressing urgency, is how to live alongside each other where the other person is our neighbour, not our competitor or disposable enemy. We are all the other to each other, a relation that sometimes descends into relegation and demonisation. This short monograph refines thinking on the subject of the *other*. In doing so, it rejects the proposition that othering, as the ascription of a pejorative status, is an inevitable feature of human life. The reader will be invited to consider that a transformative, ethically informed, political act can reduce the negative imputation of the other. If the conditions of existence under which we conduct our lives at any given moment are a contingent creation, if not a freakish biological accident (Dawkins, 2006; Harari, 2014), then the political and economic, the ethical and cultural, can be reconstructed to achieve different outcomes. Although it is necessary to frame the process and function of othering within a broad stream of history, I also include an organisational perspective from the criminal justice system. With one notable exception, there is a paucity of monographs *solely* dedicated to the other in criminal justice and penal policy. This notable exception (at the time of writing) is an edited collection on *Punishing the Other* (Eriksson, 2016), which applies Bauman's (1989) thesis on the social production of immorality to exclusion, punishment and criminalisation. It is asserted that, 'In short, this book provides a critical analysis of social distancing in action and, where appropriate, a discussion on where morality is located within such processes and outcomes' (Eriksson, 2016, p 2). The Eriksson collection contains case studies on the Other (the upper case is used throughout the text). It also reintroduces the much-needed moral dimension to criminal justice, penal policy, immigration as the control of strangers and the social process of othering. Specifically, on the moral contestation of othering, Eriksson utilises Bauman (1989), where, with traces of Schweitzer and Bonhoeffer (see Whitehead, 2015a; see also Chapter Three), the immoral is human behaviour that avoids the responsibility of the self for the other. In other words, the other is constituted as disposable enemy rather than neighbour.

It is churlish not to acknowledge the contribution of *Punishing the Other* to empirical research on, theorisation of and manifestations of the other. However, it does not go far enough towards a resolution of the problem it addresses. Consequently, there is scope to: broaden our thinking to incorporate a longer-term stream-of-history perspective; acknowledge troubling transformations imposed upon the criminal justice system by a succession of 'modernising' governments; foreground moral responses to contest the production of the relegated and demonised other; and forge a new agreement on ethical priorities to establish the conditions of existence that benefit all of us. These four themes represent the four substantive chapters of this monograph. Within the parameters of these four chapters, I will refer to the transcendental materialist perspective (see Hall, 2012), and the three orders of Imaginary, Symbolic and Real in the company of Lacan and Žižek. This will be explained later. Accordingly, it is imperative to think about the other in relation to macro (historical, political, material conditions and ideological commitments), mezzo (organisational transformations) and micro (human subjectivity), which will feature in what unfolds later. The scope most certainly exists to contest othering: to proceed from the construction and function of othering through new political and ethical commitments to change the way we organise ourselves and think about each other. Therefore, it is possible to reframe the contours of the debate and to move things on from where they reside at present.

There is also scope to produce a more nuanced theorisation of the other. Eriksson and her colleagues (Eriksson, 2016) assuredly theorise the other within the organisational context of criminal justice and penal policy. However, we should acknowledge:

- How extremist and anti-ethical ideologies have the potential to establish themselves within our neurological circuits to foster prejudice, bitterness and resentment that culminate in harms directed against others. These harms include negative attitudes towards race, disability, transgender, even facial appearance (see Chakraborti and Garland, 2015). Nevertheless, this constitutes a contingent not permanent condition of existence.
- Social distancing, the opposite of proximity, prises open the space to erode our responsibility for others (Bauman, 1989).
- Elongating the political and social hierarchy exacerbates inequality, which, in turn, weakens social bonds (Wilkinson and Pickett, 2009).
- The neoliberal capitalist order reproduces egoistic individualism, which reconfigures moral boundaries to weaken obligations towards each other. The transition from family and community to state and market (Sandel, 2012) promotes self-interest and fearful competition rather than mutual coexistence.
- Neoliberal capitalism operates amorally when it puts profit before people, economics before ethics. The system's core releases competitive forces that are harmful to how we organise, live alongside each other (Whitehead, 2015a, 2016a) and conduct our relationships.
- Biological, psychological and social deficiencies have been carved into our natures (Harari, 2014) by a contingent historical and evolutionary process. However, this is a process that can be reversed.

Furthermore, as Smith (2016, p 19) comments when discussing Nazi ideology, which I will expand upon later: 'Some of the techniques of Othering that may have helped facilitate the exterminations are related to ideology, obedience to authority, peer pressure, de-individuation, unity in primary groups and even career-based motives'. In short, this monograph is positioned in relation to Eriksson's diverse collection in order to take it forward (specifically, Chapter Two). However, I want to achieve much more than think about criminal justice. The subject matter is vital and urgent because it fundamentally and foundationally confronts all of us with how we conduct our lives alongside each other, under prevailing political and economic conditions of existence. It is as relevant for personal relations as it is for organisational functioning, as well as national, European and international relations. Arguably, we have moved into a situation where there is a greater disposition towards othering than towards the well-being and flourishing of all. It is stated that 'Human nurturing and flourishing are low on the agenda for all those who find success in the market difficult' (Hall and Winlow, 2015, p 91). Perhaps the matter can be put like this: if postmodernism constitutes the *cultural logic* of the neoliberal capitalist order (Jameson, 1991), modernising transformations in criminal justice and penal policy in general, and probation in particular, constitute the *organisational logic* of neoliberal capitalism (Whitehead, 2015a, 2016a), and the production and reproduction of the demonised and relegated other constitutes the *anthropological logic* of neoliberal conditions of existence during the early years of the 21st century. Although there are multiple causes of othering, we should not avoid confrontation with the neoliberal capitalist order and its global embrace.

Let us join the philosophers to assert that we do not really know why we exist or why there is something rather than nothing. We participate in the accidental rather than the necessary conditions of life, in addition to the complex matrix of biological, psychological and sociological variables that stake out our interactions with each other. We lack knowledge of our destiny, and the meanings we crave are not neatly packaged and then delivered by the world in which we live, but must be constructed and imposed by us. This includes how to coexist in harmonious personal relations with others, a problem acknowledged from the existentialists to Freud (Olson, 1962; Blackham, 1965). Sartre (1948) asserted that being-for-ourselves and being-for-others are of equal importance, but that individuals and nations are defined by how they relate to each other. A responsible and mature way of life is informed by our ability to distinguish the self from the other in order to establish a social order of mutual recognition and cooperation. At this early stage, I come clean by asserting that I would like to make life better for all, not maintain the privileges of the elite on the backs of the many. To realise this objective, it is necessary to interrupt the production and reproduction of the demonised and relegated other. It may readily be acknowledged that the subject of the other is not easy to negotiate, particularly when accusers lay the charge that my objectives are hopelessly idealistic, utopian, undoubtedly unrealistic and irredeemably facile. However, the position I advance confronts and contests othering, and its associated conditions of existence, in order to proceed from dystopian despair to idealistic hope. What is wrong with that? To engage in, and collude with, the pejorative demonisation and relegation of others damages all of us in the struggle for collective human existence. Accordingly, the subject matter of this book is as important as it is timely and topical.

This monograph incorporates illustrative historical compass points, anthropology and human subjectivity, our biological-material constitution, ethics and culture, the politico-economic conditions of existence, and criminal and social justice. It acknowledges that we are socialised differently, as well as the existence of religious fault lines, ethnic conflicts, prejudice and bigotry. Hegel recognised, as did Durkheim, that ethics is a question of political and social organisation rather than a collection of isolated individual wills in competition with each other (see Eagleton 2009, p 126). The more detached we are from each other, facilitated by elongating the pyramidal socio-economic hierarchy (Wilkinson and Pickett, 2009), the more likely we will construct the demonised, relegated and excluded other. The well-being of each person is the platform for the fulfilment of all of us and, as Eagleton (2009, p 126) rightly asserts, it is difficult to think of a more important form of ethics and culture. This ethical position resonates with Bertrand Russell's (1946, p 710) comment articulated in the gendered convention of the 1940s: 'Man is not a solitary animal, and so long as social life survives, self-realisation cannot be the supreme principle of ethics'. This monograph is playfully exploratory, sometimes more theoretical than pragmatic, but it does consider a future different to the past and present.

We have much to explore in the next four chapters on the subject of the other, as well as formulating a resolution, which is urgently required and has contemporary significance for all of us. A good place to start is to step into the stream of history to frame, scope and illustrate the problem. In doing so, I could be charged with a lack of balance, of assembling a biased picture. However, I am deliberately selective to illustrate the theme of the other that attracts evidential support from the historical record.

ONE

Framing the other: stepping into the stream of history

A biological springboard

The weight of evidence shoring up the historical record strongly suggests that Homo sapiens have not afforded themselves the opportunity to live alongside each other under conditions of a shared global ethic or moral economy (see Götz, 2015). The earth began to form 4.5 billion years ago, long before the appearance of the genus Homo 2.5 million years ago. Neanderthals can be traced back 500,000 years, and Homo sapiens 200,000 years. These evolutionary staging posts occurred long before the Agricultural Revolution of 12,000 years ago that signalled the domestication of plants and animals. This made it possible, for the first time, to establish permanent human settlements. Prior to this tipping point that decisively altered the course of human life on earth, our ancestors lived in small groups as hunter-gatherers. Subsequently, the ability to grow crops to sustain life in a permanent location presented the challenge of how to exist in 'mass cooperation networks, when they lacked the biological instincts to sustain such networks' (Harari, 2014, p 133). It is suggested that Homo sapiens were not endowed with the biological equipment to live alongside each other in conditions of mutual coexistence. There was no essential human nature predisposed towards cooperation. This was manifested as towns and cities grew bigger, and early civilisations expanded their frontiers through flexing their imperialistic muscles, toned by violence towards others. Consequently, over recent millennia, the self has struggled to live with the other, nation alongside nation, in universal cooperation networks. We are up against it to discover a period of history that prioritised people before profit, ethics before economics, and the collective interest before national self-interest, under conditions of equality and mutual respect for the lives of others.

If we follow the explanation sketched by Harari (2014), it is suggested that our biological inability to achieve cooperative human relations was compensated for by cultivating shared myths or imaginary scripts. These myths and scripts – religious world views, belief systems and structures of meaning and value – were the ingredients that facilitated the transition from raw nature to human culture. Psychoanalytically speaking, this was the transition from the Real to the Symbolic in order to impose a facade of meaning and purpose that enabled people to live together.[1] We will return to what this means later. Accordingly, Harari (2014, p 163) refers to the construction of artificial instincts to enable strangers to cooperate with each other in towns and cities. He also states, pertinent to this book, that Homo sapiens have cleaved humanity into 'we' and 'they', 'us' and 'them' (Harari, 2014, p 195), an observation that receives support by peeling back the historical record. This cleaving of humanity into 'us' and 'them' resonates with the theme of the other, which can be clarified by considering the following terms of reference:

- *Other* – the name ascribed to the relegated and demonised, for example, minority ethnic groups and people who offend, in order to signify difference from the law-abiding and lawmakers.
- *Othering* – the process that culminates in appending the name of the *other*. It alludes to procedural steps in the application, imputation and imposition of the *other* through a process of reassignment.

- *Othered* – the aforementioned process culminates in the designation of the *other*, the confirmation of a relegated and demonised status.
- *Otherness* – the quality or condition of being different once the pejorative designation has been imposed.
- *Other* as function – the application of positive qualities to oneself at the expense of negative qualities imputed to the *other*. The function of the *other* should be excavated under specific politico-economic arrangements, or play of forces. The *other* functions to 'supply an important service to society by patrolling the outer edges of group space and by providing a contrast which gives the rest of the community some sense of their own territorial identity' (Erikson, 1966, p 196). Moreover, its function can serve to divert attention away from structural or political-economic problems (Katz, 1989) by pathologising the individual.
- *Contesting the other* – the preceding schematisation should include the moral contestation of othering, which we will consider later in Chapter Three.

Some evidence from the historical record

Exploring the other, albeit briefly, should be framed within a fast-flowing stream of history. Hall (2012) refers to merchant adventurers 1,000 years ago in pursuit of commercial advantages (see also Ackroyd, 2011). The historical record can be pushed further back to the Roman Empire, where adventurers and traders plundered their way across the Mediterranean for centuries (Beard, 2015, p 199; see also Holland, 2015). Beard lends support to Frankopan (2015) in drawing attention to commercial opportunities derived from conquests, the slave, spice and cotton trades, and seizing booty and plunder. In fact, the world of 1st-century Rome was one of brutal interstate violence, the legacy of Alexander's conquests (Beard, 2015, p 194). This 'classical age' of Macedon, Greece and Rome followed Egypt, Assyria, Babylonia and Persia, ribboned alongside the Nile, Tigris and Euphrates. These nations were familiar with repeated bouts of interstate conflict in pursuit of their own imperialistic ambitions. For some to win, others had to lose.

The foundation myth of Rome offered a welcome to foreigners, runaways and criminals. Nevertheless, the Roman state was a hierarchically structured social order with patricians and plebeians, free and slave, men and women, haves and have-nots, Roman citizens and outsiders, wealthy and poor, powerful and powerless, and the accepted and relegated. These binary distinctions were determined by accident of birth, allocated rank, by which human beings were sieved, graded and fixed within a historically contingent social order (Holland, 2015, p 9). This coffee-bean selection process of human beings has repeated itself many times throughout the historical record. Whatever moral fibre existed within Roman culture was 'destroyed by the city's success and by the wealth, greed and lust for power that had followed its conquest of the Mediterranean and the crushing of all its serious rivals' (Beard, 2015, p 38). Roman culture, and, before this, Alexander's Macedonian empire, put a high value on conflict so that 'Prowess, bravery and deadly violence in battle were repeatedly celebrated' (Beard, 2015, p 162). All empires, from those just cited to the British Empire and the US, were founded on, expanded through and sustained by the threat and exercise of violence, with a high value placed on military might. Nation building and self-aggrandisement, persistently pursued at the expense of the lives of others considered of dubious value, is a recurring feature. However, then, as now, there was always the possibility of ethical and cultural contestation, for example, as with Seneca, for whom the 'prosperity that was the mark of a great empire was, in his opinion, a treacherous and soul-destroying thing, characterised by perpetual restlessness, and destined only to torment itself' (Holland, 2015, p 366). However, this moral questioning requires qualification because Seneca was compromised by his association with the Emperor Nero, who was hardly a commendable role model for a sustainable ethical lifestyle. It is also worth mentioning that social distinction within Roman society was challenged by the Athenian experiment in equality during the 7th and 6th centuries BCE (Scott, 2016, p 66; see also Jaspers, 1953).

If 1st-century Rome was characterised by interstate violence, the Empire was, in turn, destroyed by violence. When the Germanic invaders from the north flooded southwards during the 4th and 5th centuries CE, there was no peaceful transition of power. For the Germanic male, violence was a manifestation of duty and a source of pleasure that inscribed the stigmata of status (Ward-Perkins, 2005, p 49), just as war was the highest duty and greatest achievement of monarchs (Ackroyd, 2011, p 322). From the Germanic invasions to the depredations of Viking invaders during the 11th century, followed, in turn, by the violent interposition of Norman hegemony, particularly in Northern England (Ackroyd, 2011, p 82), monuments have been erected to the inability of Homo sapiens to live together as one people (on Medieval economy and society, 1100–1500, see Postan, 1972; on the 'vital century', 1714–1815, see Rule, 1995). Claims to superior status and lording it over others, even the doctrine of divine rights, have militated against one universal humanity.

The Venetian Empire between the 12th and 16th centuries carved out trade routes stimulated by financial calculation, commodities and business enterprises, sustained and expanded by ruthless competition. During these centuries, Venice functioned as a precursor of the capitalist system, propelled forward by the Dutch during the 18th century, London in the 19th century with investment capital accrued from the slave trade, the US in the 20th century and, more recently, Brazil, Russia, India, China, and South Africa (the BRICS) during the early years of the 21st century. Venice was positioned at the strategic geopolitical hub of an extensive trading empire throughout the Adriatic and Black Sea, where almost everything was up for sale. The profit premium generated desire over need, and ethics and culture followed the accountant's logic. The capitalist order of things that structures our lives did not erupt *ex nihilo* fully formed after the 1780s or even earlier. There are richly layered archaeological deposits that signposted future incursions, some of which we are considering here. By the 19th century, we find that John Ruskin contested the ugly monstrosities of Victorian capitalism, asserted that there is *no wealth but life* and hankered after living conditions, more imagined than real, that were presumed to exist before the Victorian era (Batchelor, 2000). Similarly, Thompson (1971) referred to paternalistic arrangements before the 18th century, subsequently eroded by the egoistic individualism of industrial capitalism. Nevertheless, if Ruskin and Thompson had pushed back their historical purview, they would have encountered compelling evidence of violent competition conducted in pursuit of national self-interest over innumerable centuries, power struggles, the relentless pursuit of commercial interests and trade routes between East and West that opened up markets in furs, cotton, silk, spices, silver and gold, as well as human bodies (Frankopan, 2015; see also Riello, 2013). These were the staple activities of imperial adventurers, empire builders and power brokers that prized material advancement more than valued moral economy, universal ethics and equality. Hegel (1770–1831) may well have believed that history was imbued with a divine purpose (see Singer, 1983). Nevertheless, this optimistic interpretation distorted an empirical record of relentless international barbarism that relegated and demonised countless others.

Remaining in the 19th century, England was the most industrialised country in the world, its restless energies stoked by laissez-faire economics, utilitarian philosophy and evangelical religion that congealed to fashion a human subject replete with individualism. The industrial system advanced through capital accumulation with the economic benefit of constant expansion and reinvestment. However, it damaged social and ethical relations, as understood by Ruskin and Thompson. Political economy moved forward under the tutelage of private ownership, commodities bought and sold in a competitive marketplace for commercial advantage, and surplus value extracted from the labour force of industrial capitalism. Although Max Weber romanticised the capitalist spirit when extolling the virtues of work as a religious calling and material success as the mark of divine favour, Durkheim and Marx appreciated that the essential core of the system weakened moral economy and social stability. By the 1880s, numerous changes and crises elicited ameliorative responses to the capitalist order of things, which culminated in the reforming New Liberals of 1906–14. The argument surfaced, sustained by an emerging body of empirical evidence, that the capitalist spirit was accompanied by disruptive ethical and social effects requiring regulatory intervention. It was a system that did not help human beings to live together in cooperative networks. Nevertheless, economic tribulations and periodic crises persisted throughout the early decades of the 20th century, and the interwar years in the UK and US discredited the ability of the capitalist order to deliver political, economic and social stability. Although there were signs of economic recovery by 1924, six years after the end of the First World War (Kershaw, 2015), the Wall Street crash of October 1929 and the 1930s' Great Depression nevertheless conjured the feeling that capitalism was in terminal crisis. Insensate capitalism preyed upon human beings with a pitiless relentlessness but there was, and remains, the possibility of an alternative world view that would reduce the harms we inflict upon each other.

A series of historical events, briefly recounted earlier, reaching back throughout centuries of human history, were eventually sucked into the expanding capitalist system by the 19th century. Consequently, the dominant motif of life on earth is not so much the progressive march of a *civilising process* to bring us closer to each other (Elias, 1994), but rather a *pseudo-pacification process* (Hall, 2012, 2014). Repetitive historical cycles, eternal recurrences of ruthless competition and intra-national and international conflict to maintain a material advantage over others did not wither away by a progressive evolutionary process towards enlightened civilisation and harmonious social relations. Although it was necessary to curb excessive forms of violence through ethico-social relations in order to create stable trading conditions for the capitalist enterprise to flourish, its core required aggressive forms of competition. Therefore, if it is possible to appeal to the record of history to demonstrate a decline in violence over recent centuries, the insight of the *pseudo-pacification theory* is that this was not a result of a civilising process, but, rather, the emergence of 'a dualistic economic need for pacification in an emerging market economy' (Hall and Winlow, 2015, p 116). The kernel of the *pseudo-pacification theory* is the sublimation of violence and aggression that was converted into a functionally aggressive yet practical rule-bound competition for wealth and status represented by the preening display of socio-symbolic objects in a burgeoning consumer culture (for a detailed exposition of this theory, see Hall and Winlow, 2015, pp 115–20).

A character in Sebastian Faulks' novel *Where my heart used to beat* enriches the theme of the other: "'What's interesting'", I said, "is how the [20th] century made it possible for educated Europeans – people who had given birth to the Renaissance and the Enlightenment – to come to think that individual life is, without intrinsic value'" (Faulks, 2015, p 127). Prior to the 20th century, it was possible to believe, notwithstanding the barbarities of ancient civilisations and imperialistic adventures, that the world was becoming more humane, more enlightened, lending support to Hegel's optimistic reading of the historical process (see Singer, 1983). However, Ypres, Loos and the Somme nailed the lie of a civilisation process. The Venetian Empire may well have been in decline for centuries, and the British Empire turned into a commonwealth of nations, but the capitalist spirit of recent centuries, stimulated by exchange relations and competitive conflicts, reproduces psychosocial restlessness and the 'anxiety-driven fetish of consumer symbolism in the construction of identity and the achievement of status' (Hall, 2012, p 247). These are the conditions of existence within which to explore pejorative othering: seeing the other person as our competitor and disposable enemy rather than neighbour. Of course, we have managed to do much more that relegate and demonise each other, but our ability to do so is supported by this brief excursion into the historical record.

Brief respite: some positive usages

The subject of the other is of central importance for all of us. Predominantly, I am excavating the negative construction of the other. It is also of interest to include a criminal justice and penal policy organisational perspective (see Chapter Two). However, this is not its only usage. The other can also be alluring by drawing us into the lives of others as a source of enrichment. Here, the *other* conveys assimilation with another person to participate in what has been described as a 'fantastic world of otherness' that transcends the limitations of one's own life (Carey, 2014, p 34). The other can be a positive role model worthy of respect, or someone simply better than us at academic excellence or athletic ability. This should elicit a magnanimous response rather than resentment; it could even inspire us to raise our own game. The philosopher David Hume (1711–76) rounded on Hobbes (1588–1679), who said that Homo sapiens are basically self-interested. Instead, argued Hume, human beings have the capacity to take pleasure in the flourishing of *others*: there are a thousand instances that are the 'marks of a general benevolence in human nature' (Hume, 1983 [1777], p 92). Similarly, Adam Smith (1723–90), at the cusp of the *great transformation* of industrial capitalism, believed an *invisible hand* would ensure that self-interest benefited the general interest of *others* (he was mistaken about this). The dictum was: attend to the business of generating profit consistent with the demands of capitalism and the public good takes care of itself.[2] Human beings indubitably engage in self-interested activities but, like Hume, Smith (2009 [1759]) considered that they are capable of demonstrating an interest in the happiness of *others*. So, the pejorative reading of the other, the process and functioning of othering, does not get all its own way.

The novelist James Joyce considered that human growth is possible through openness towards the *other* (Kiberd, 2009, p 246). George Eliot thought that the world can be a better place if we make the effort to comprehend the *other* (Mead, 2014, p 223). If we emulate the novelists, it benefits ethical and social relations, promotes the bonds of social solidarity, and lubricates the circuits of moral economy. It could also make us feel better about ourselves by taking us out of ourselves towards the *other* in order to make the world a better place by being attentive to the well-being of all (Whitehead, 2015a). The *other*, constitutive of ethical duty and obligation, is Sartre's 'being-for-others' and Schweitzer's reverence for life. Duty and obligation for the *other* direct us towards a politics of universality 'that cuts across the social field to create new forms of attachment, community and recognition' (Winlow et al, 2015, p 133), which are more productive and life-enhancing than the pursuit of self-interest. However, illustrations culled from the historical record cited earlier, in addition to the workings of the global capitalist system that structures our lives, have created the pejorative *other* through attaching primary significance to economics, not ethics: relations of exchange and marketised competition that produce 'winners' and 'losers' under contingent conditions of existence.

Paul Theroux (2015, p 401) discloses a revealing exchange during his travels in the *Deep South* of the US on the subject of capitalist economics and banking as a white monopoly. Theroux was told by a group of black farmers in Fargo, Arkansas:

'Thing you've got to understand' Andre said, and thought a moment before he proceeded. 'Bankers give other farmers more'.

'What other farmers'? I asked.

Andre widened his eyes and blew out his cheeks but said nothing.

'You can speak freely to Mr. Paul' Dr. King said.

'By other I mean white'.

The subject of the *other* can be explored from different perspectives. It conveys the designation of difference, an oppositional and contrary category that conjures up something otherwise than it should be. It draws attention to the binary distinction of self–other, I–you, us–them, good–bad and positive–negative judgements. Essentially, the *other* is an ascribed mark of demarcation that can be situated along a continuum from the individual and family, to community, region, nation and race. It is also applicable to organisational practices, which we will come to later, and is illuminated by a fast-flowing stream of history. Othering, according to Harari (2014), is a consequence of biological deficiencies. However, it can also be explained by faulty socialisation, harmful ideologies, the fault lines perpetuated by extremist religions and politico-economic systems that exclude more than assimilate (see

Wilkinson and Pickett, 2009). Othering is manifested in raw prejudice and bigotry. Illustrations of the other are innumerable, from Nazi ideology to the contemporary refugee crisis in Europe (Žižek, 2016), as well as the criminal justice system, which constitutes a revealing case study in demonisation and relegation. Finally, and importantly, the practices of othering can be ethically contested, which is explored in Chapter Three. The construction of the demonised *other*, whatever its origin, is a deeply troubling activity that must be contested, which is a central concern of this monograph. After stepping into the stream of history to explore essential features appertaining to the subject, let us turn to three detailed illustrations.

First illustration from the 20th century: Nazi tyranny

The first illustration of the *other* is located at the extremity of human experience. It defies rational explanation by the heirs of the European Enlightenment, liberal progressives and supporters of a civilisation process. This notable illustration is the jackbooted, black-shirted, goose-stepping, moustachioed-led Nazi tyranny during the 1930s and 1940s, accessed ethnographically through Gill (1988), a novel by Amis (2015) and (on the *Nazi Concentration Camps* or *konzentrationslager* [KL]) Wachsmann (2015). In a previous publication, Amis (2000) stated that Auschwitz-Birkenau is beyond belief precisely because it demonstrates barbarism on an industrial scale: the contempt of one person against another, one racial group against another, one political ideology set against a religious culture (see Anderson, 1988; see also Chapter Three). Ideologically, it operated at the infantile tabloid level but ideology translated into concerted action in a destructive display of ferocity directed against adults and children some 20 years after the trench-ridden, mud-clinging and bullet-strafing human catastrophe of 1914–18. This was a moral horror, a revolting aesthetic (Tyler, 2013, p 25). Nazi ideology constructed numerous categories of the relegated *other*: anti-social typologies, gypsies, delinquents, criminals, homosexuals, Jehovah's Witnesses, priests, political opponents, communists, socialists, Poles and Slavs in the East, freemasons, Jews, beggars, pimps, the homeless, female prostitutes, the sick, weak, incurable and infectious, and 'cripples'. Ruthless action:

> was required against criminals, political enemies, and other deviants who might attack the regime. During a time of crisis, Hitler repeated again and again, one had to exterminate, eliminate, execute, beat to death, shoot, liquidate large numbers of scum, rats, and asocial vermin. (Wachsmann, 2015, p 415)

The camps that can be traced to 1933–34 were essential for the disposal of numerous categories of the *other* (on Nazi othering, see Smith, 2016; on scapegoats and the other, see Winlow et al, 2016, p 165).

The rationale that structured the naming, process, designation and function of the *other* was the Nazi evaluation of unorthodox behaviour according to blood, stock and racial purity. Membership of the incorrect human stock attracted the designation of *Untermenschen* (subhuman), a grotesque travesty of universal humanity. Specifically, Jews were juxtaposed with profit and greed, and blamed for recent economic catastrophes. The Jewish nation was fascistically scapegoated as *other* from which the Nazi state required ritual purification through state-sponsored cathartic displays of hatred and violence, after which all would be well in the European continent. Prior to the Nazi state in Germany, Jews had been the subject of Russian pogroms in the East. Additionally, following the catastrophe of the First World War, the search for scapegoats was pursued with alacrity, which cultivated fertile ground for the spread of hatred and prejudice. Accordingly, the multifaceted image of Jews was sharpened as the 'enemy of Christianity, capitalist exploiter, shirker of military duty, fomenter of internal unrest, driving force of Bolshevism' (Kershaw, 2015, p 78). The camps that accommodated *Untermenschen* operated a colour-scheme stigmata of the *other*: black = asocial, blue = émigré, brown = gypsy, green = criminal, mauve = Jehovah's Witnesses, pink = homosexuals, red = political, and yellow triangle = Jews (see also Jütte, 1994, p 161). Colour stigmata were complemented by the digitisation of the *other* as Jews were tattooed on the left forearm, the indelible signage of *othering*.

Primo Levi (1987) described his own demolition and pejorative relegation upon entering the camps. He recounts how he was branded with the number 174517 on his left arm. Prior to the camps, Gill (1988, p 29) says that 'Several Jews in the ghetto were in fact branded on the forehead with the Star of David or the Swastika'. The ghetto was not a Nazi invention as evidence can be adduced of Jewish ghettos during the Middle Ages (the Venice ghetto is now a tourist destination). They were reinvented during the Nazi period to name, process and designate categories of the other (Wachsmann, 2015).

Gill's qualitative text recounts the voices of and schematic construction of the *other*. Amis honours his literary debt to Gill by revealing that this was the text that enabled him to commune 'with the presences in Gill's book, with their stoicism, eloquence, aphoristic wisdom, humour, poetry, and uniformly high level of perception' (Amis, 2015, p 305), which inspired his fictional reconstruction of the Holocaust. Gill also provides evidence on the return from being *othered* and shedding the negatively imputed status, with all its psychosocial implications – that is, from the *othering* of psychic disintegration to reconstruction and survival. Surviving the psychic trauma of the camps depended upon retaining a sense of humour when life expectancy was approximately three months, adaptability, forming small self-help groups, sliding under the radar, obtaining 'soft jobs' if possible and maintaining a sense of self, dignity, decency and integrity as a human being (Gill, 1988, p 9). However, it was extremely difficult to make the transition back to 'normal' life from the rhythmic barbarity of the camps. There would be no seamless return to a previous existence as it was impossible to be the same person before the traumatic encounter with the camps. There was no 'closure' (an inaccurate Americanism assimilated into the language), and no eradication of the ghosts from the past and dark shadows of the present, only degrees of adjustment and maladjustment (see account in Sands, 2016). This was the ultimate journey into and back and forth from hell. Othering reaches into the present with various forms of hate crimes (see Chakraborti and Garland, 2015).

More recently, Wacquant (2001) meshed prison and ghetto, class and race, in the US to expose a carceral complex for the imposition of surveillance, training and segregation in order to neutralise offenders by racial category. This constitutes the segregation and confinement of a racialised *other* in US prisons under conditions of neoliberal market capitalism. It can be observed that the USA's first black president appears to have done little to address this overrepresentation while in office. Wacquant excavates the racial and cultural function of the prison, rather than its material and economic function articulated in the *prison–industrial complex* thesis. Paul Theroux (2015) picks up the theme of racial division that persists in the US set against the explanatory backdrop of American slavery in the Southern states. Theroux (2015, p 78) makes the point that there remain places that are insular, with prosperity next to some of the worst poverty in the US, identities fixed in time by race and class, well-heeled and poor areas, and locations where "'the other side of the tracks" is not an abstract metaphor but a specific place as well as a condition and a social class'. Theroux alludes to the Ku Klux Klan, where, in the South, they evoked a violent response to the racial other in defence of a threatened white social status. The Klan originated in the mid-19th century among the planter class. Terror and violence were exercised to keep black people working in the fields, regulate labour and maintain the South's repressive plantation system (see also Asim, 2007; for those interested in the history of slavery and the racial other, see Thomas, 1998). Winlow et al (2015) refer to the *other* appertaining to race, nationality and immigration. The contemporary situation is that neoliberal capitalism, supported by its cultural logic of postmodernism, encourages us to 'shrug off all forms of collective identity and embrace an image of ourselves as unique and distinct from those others who would have once formed our political community' (Winlow et al, 2015, p 75). This is a suitable point at which to turn from our first illustration of the relegated and demonised other located in the 20th century to the current preoccupation with the ongoing refugee crisis.

Second illustration from the 21st century: refugee migrations and forced expulsions

The second illustration is graphically introduced by the late A.A Gill's (2015) journalistic account of the migrant crisis in the Balkans. His insightful observations come from Idomeni railway station, situated on the border between Greece and Macedonia. It was a transit point for Syrian refugees travelling from East to West. Exhausted refugees that Gill observed were bellowed at by Macedonian Special Forces, accompanied by the paraphernalia of truncheons and handguns. Searchlights sprayed their piercing light, refugees organised into lines and soldiers loaded railway carriages with human cargo. The lottery of escape, the crushing mass of bodies, the shouting, barking, chaos and terror of families, and the smirking and strutting soldiery, Gill proceeds with sensitivity when adding to the historical record:

> There is something about this moment, in this filthy field, with the clutching of children and luggage that conjures up a ghostly remembrance. Not mine, but ours, the continents'. This was never supposed to happen again. Never. Soldiers cramming frightened and beaten, humiliated and dehumanised others into trains, clutching their mortal goods, to be driven off into the night. (Gill, 2015, p 26)

Žižek (2016) analyses the refugee phenomenon in his book, which carries the subtitle *Refugees, terror and other troubles with the neighbours*. Importantly, he meshes the presenting problem of refugees with the impact of global capitalism. Refugee migrations from East to West is about not simply a collection of failed states and their internal disputes in Syria, Iraq, Lebanon, Libya, Somalia and the Congo, but the underbelly of global capitalist operations. Žižek argues that global capitalism promotes itself as the guarantor of human liberty and freedom in order to maintain a distinctive set of hegemonic conditions of existence (Žižek, 2016, p 51). However, dig below its surface appeal and the system reproduces itself in new forms of human slavery in the Saudi peninsula, workers in Asian sweatshops and those controlled by violent gangmasters, forced labour in the Congo, and a Chinese-owned clothing factory in Prato, Italy. The global capitalist system is empirically indexed by slavery and apartheid, which can be added to earlier illustrations of the relegated, demonised and excluded other (see also United Nations Office on Drugs and Crime, 2016). There remain pejorative human categories contingent upon specific conditions of political and economic existence.

After locating the causes of the refugee crisis in political economy, Žižek (2016, p 103) proceeds to argue that the European continent has an immediate ethical responsibility for the dignified survival of refugees. The alternative is a precipitous descent into barbarism. To put this differently, there is a moral obligation to respond, here and now, to a pressing human situation. Furthermore, there must be a longer-term strategic response to transform the conditions of existence that create refugees and facilitate pejorative othering. If we refuse to apply ourselves to both dimensions and look the other way – *the problem of the other is for others to resolve, not us* – we will destroy any hope of coexisting with each other (I will return to the dual aspects of moral obligation in the final chapter). Let us not shy away from admitting that Homo sapiens have a limitless capacity to heap harm upon harm upon each other, then blame it on what are often presented as law-like conditions or market mechanisms operating independently of human judgement and decision-making. This convoluted logic is used to justify the current order of things and avoids accepting our moral obligation to replace it in order to reduce pejorative othering.

Third illustration: the end of the post-war European project?

The UK went to the polls on 23 June 2016 to vote on whether to remain within or exit the European Union. After decades of unresolved tensions in the UK's relation with Europe, particularly but not exclusively from within the Conservative Party, the vote was a defining but arguably dangerous moment. We should recall that Ted Heath secured British membership of the then Common

Market in 1973. This was followed by a referendum in June 1975 under Wilson's Labour government, when 68.7% (14,918,009) voted to remain and 31.3% (6,812,052) voted to leave. Only two out of 47 voting areas voted to leave the Common Market: Shetlands and the Western Isles. Run the tape forward to the summer of 2016 and the outcome was too close to call but favoured the Brexiteers: 51.9% leave (17,410,000) votes; 48.1% remain (16,141,000 votes). The sometimes unedifying arguments and populist sentiments were framed largely by competitive economics – 'We'll be materially "better off" outside Europe'. Unfortunately, being 'better off' cannot be quantified by this striking illustration of wing-and-prayer economics. When excavating the referendum result from a national, pan-European and international perspective, it is a victory for insular nationalism rather than one universal European continent. The vote was a serious blow to the European political project for closer integration from a generation located at a considerable distance from the First and Second World Wars (Juncker, 2015). Tim Shipman's (2016, p 581) insightful book on the political fallout of Brexit reflects the position that the referendum signalled a breakdown of trust between rulers and ruled, an outbreak of paranoia and even a 'fear of the other, whether that person is foreign or black or whatever it might be'. The vote floated to the surface the national concern with immigration (see Shipman, 2016, pp 293, 457) and reignited, yet again, the grumbling threat of Scottish independence.

Britain's decision to leave the European Union could tempt other nations to rush towards the exit. However, in 2016, Austria rejected a far-right head of state; in March 2017, the Dutch rejected the far-right candidate Geert Wilders for prime minister; and the French presidential election campaign in May 2017 resulted in defeat for Marine Le Pen, who would have taken France out of the European Union. The European vote in the UK is a troubling story of separation, division, fragmentation and an expensive divorce settlement that raises questions pertinent to the process and functioning of othering. The selective historical record that we looked at earlier provides evidence for human beings and nations being sieved, graded, classified, demonised, relegated and sometimes vomited out. Also, over recent decades, there were Russian pogroms directed against Jewish people, Stalin's purges and gulag, Mao's anti-ethico-cultural revolution, Pol Pot's Cambodian genocide, and the disturbing tremors of European nationalism creating a narrow-minded particularism rather than extolling a life-enhancing vision of universal ethics and one humanity (see also Chomsky, 2016). These extreme and selective illustrations of constructing the pejorative other do not constitute the totality of human experience. Nevertheless, they remind us of our responsibility to learn the lessons that past events can teach us, and to be on our guard against those dangers that threaten our collective humanity, social solidarity and ethical universalism. After wading in the stream of history and providing three detailed vignettes, I now turn to the expansion and reproduction of the demonised and relegated other in the modernised criminal justice system and penal policy, in other words, to a more focused organisational illustration of the demonised other.

Notes

[1]   Although I expand on the three psychic orders of Imaginary, Symbolic and Real later, an early sketch is appropriate here. According to Lacanian psychoanalysis, human beings exist in three dimensions or orders. The *Imaginary* is 'our direct lived experience of reality, but also of our dreams and nightmares – it is the domain of appearing, of how things appear to us' (Žižek, 2014, p 119). The *Symbolic Order/Big Other* is the invisible order that structures our experience of reality, networks of codes, rules, meanings and culture, which make us see how we see – a filter, sieve, socially constructed and imposed order of existence. The *Real* is the pre-symbolic and is associated with trauma, shock and violence; it destabilises, disturbs and can destroy our universe of meaning. Accordingly, 'the Real can only be discerned in its traces, effects or aftershocks' (Žižek, 2014, p 120).

[2]   In addition to Adam Smith, we can also mention the French physiocrats – Quesnay (1694–1774) and Turgot (1727–81). The central economic and scientific tenet of the physiocrats was the existence of economic laws and so economic progress depended on their unfettered operation. Governments must not interfere in the working of these laws and not restrict competition or the natural order of things will be interrupted.

TWO

Criminalising the other: a criminal justice excursus

With one notable exception mentioned earlier (Eriksson, 2016), there are no monographs dedicated *solely* to the subject of criminal justice and the offending other, which is a surprising academic omission. However, the subject of the other is a sub-theme coursing through a number of texts, including Becker (1963) on *outsiders*, Cohen (1973) on *folk devils*, Jütte (1994) on the *stigmatised* and Bauman (2004) on *wasted lives and outcasts* (for a contemporary reading of the *scapegoat*, see also Winlow et al, 2016). In other words, there are scattered deposits, located within disparate intellectual resources, waiting to be garnered and then flushed to the surface to forge a synthesis of the subject. I would like to present a brief literature review of these resources on the demonised and relegated other in criminal justice and penal policy.

Criminological resources on the demonised other

Garland (2001, p 137) refers to a *criminology of the other* along two axes. First, offenders are just like us, indistinguishable from the law-abiding. The only difference between the law-abiding and lawbreaking is that the latter have failed to exercise the quality of reason that would prevent recourse to criminality. Given the correct calibration of rational choice and deterrent punishment, criminal behaviour can be avoided (the principle of classical criminology). Second, 'scientific' positivism constructs the image of dangerous predators lurking in the shadows, the harmful and risky who pose a threat to civilised life in the city. So, essentially, not like us at all. Positivism ascribes to offenders an ontological otherness (biological, psychological, sociological), a different essence, discoverable by the appliance of science and the finely calibrated instruments of quantitative measurement. This is a 'scientific' approach that involves the application of numbers to people snagged by the criminal justice system, in addition to the aforementioned *konzentrationslager*. Rodger expands the category of offending behaviour to include 'chavs', those not in education, employment or training (NEETs), and the underclass of late-capitalist modernity. They have been described as the 'willful deviants who behave in an anti-social way because they fail to take the opportunities and make the choices that would benefit them most' (Rodger, 2008, p 69). Cook (2006) clearly asserts that the criminal justice system constructs the deviant *other*. It achieves this outcome by criminalising what are socio-structural problems under neoliberal capitalist arrangements, and it then segregates and excludes in an expanded prison system that deflects the real source of the problem – in other words, individualising, problematising and pathologising what are fundamentally issues and questions associated with the prevailing political and economic conditions of existence.

Young (2007) explores the *genesis of 'othering'*. Genesis and process involve ascribing a superior status to oneself according to the master categories of class, gender, race, nationality and religion, accompanied by imputing negative qualities to *others*. The cognate features of naming, process, designation and function are applied to trade unions, the unemployed, scroungers, delinquents and benefit cheats but, take note, less vigorously to tax avoiders, even though they arguably inflict greater harms on others. Young elucidates *conservative demonisation*, which ascribes positive attributes to the self and imputes negative qualities to others. By contrast, *liberal othering* is where the *other* is deemed to lack our qualities and virtues, which can be compensated. This does not convey essential or innate qualitative differences, but rather a deficit, a lacking, caused by material and cultural deprivation that can be remedied by the right social policies. Katz (1989, pp 5–6) nails the lie of Young's conservative demonisation, and Garland's essentialist axis, when stating that 'By mistaking socially constructed categories for natural distinctions, we reinforce inequality and stigmatise even those we set out to help'.

Bell (2011) directs attention to the consequences of New Labour's criminal justice policies between 1997 and 2010 (also Whitehead, 2016a), characterised by more punishment and prison, surveillance and criminal law hyperinflation. This process began in earnest under Michael Howard and John Major around 1992–93, and then continued after 1997, initiating criminological and criminal justice trends that have been 'accompanied by the rise of a discourse about the crime problem which tends to demonise offenders and potential offenders … thus exacerbating their exclusion from mainstream society' (Bell, 2011, p 114). Reiner (2007) explores the ethical harms imposed by neoliberal competitive market societies that make it difficult to exercise responsibility for each other. Importantly, Reiner embeds othering in the conditions of existence created by the neoliberal order of things because it elevates individualism above social solidarity. Standing (2011) agrees with Young (2007) that those who endorse the ideological and material tenets of neoliberal capitalism ignore the construction of the *other* embedded within a politico-economic order that undermines universal economic security. In other words, the imputation of a negative otherness does not reflect some essential and innate difference. Rather, individuals, families, groups and communities bear the stigmata of market society imposed from above, the stigmata of the capitalist organisation of how we live together. Therefore, the orthodox analysis of crime 'emphasises agency over structure and management of the administration of life's difficulties over the structural inequalities which generate these difficulties' (Young, 2007, p 112). When excavating the concept of the *other*, it is helpful to recall what MacIntyre (1967, p 200) said about Hegel on human subjectivity: 'What passions and what ends the individual has and can have are a matter of the kind of social structure in which the individual finds himself. Desires are elicited and specified by the objects presented to them' (see also the conceptual framework of Lacan and Žižek alluded to earlier and expanded on later in connection with transcendental materialism).

Murray (1984, 1990, 1994) dispenses with any pretence to sociological subtlety when boldly advancing the interpretation of certain forms of behaviour rooted in ethico-cultural dereliction, not explanation by recourse to the politico-economic structure imposed *from above*. In other words, *othering* is predominantly a self-imposed or self-selected status for which the individual must assume sole responsibility. Murray ignores the lessons of history, as well as classical (Durkheim, Weber and Marx) and contemporary (Harrington, 2005; Hall, 2012) excursions into sociological theory on the impact of material forces, deregulated markets and differential opportunity structures. In doing so, individuals are abstracted from their political, economic and social context. According to Murray's myopic view of the world, criminality manifests a lack of moral fibre, personal weakness and faulty values. What other rational explanation could there be for the presence of the *other*? For the authoritarian 'Right' in the US and UK, the underclass of conservative criminology involves young people, homelessness, illegitimacy, crime, abuse, drugs, single mothers, promiscuity and beggars. These are the tightly clustered isobars of underclass formation and representation. For the 'Left', such behavioural manifestations mask deep politico-economic transformations associated with neoliberal capitalism since the 1980s. The shift from the Keynesian to the neoliberal order (through Hayek, Friedman, Thatcher, Reagan, Blair, Brown and the Coalition government in 2010) was responsible for the 'deterioration in the material conditions which generate social marginality for disadvantaged social groups' (Rodger, 2008, p 53). Murray repairs to the US and UK to advance the *underclass thesis* and its proffered solution, which perversely, but consistent with his world view, is to abolish the assistantial social-welfare state in order to eradicate fecklessness and dependency. Murray's analysis and prescription resonate with the undeserving poor thesis of the 19th century. Early to mid-Victorian thought conceptualised poverty as a product of defective character, not environment – an ethical and cultural, not economic, issue. Nevertheless, it is of interest to note that intellectual transformations occurred from the 1880s, as neatly captured by Stedman-Jones (1971, p 286) in *Outcast London*:

> The theory of poverty that emerged from this literature differed significantly from the literature of the 1860s and 1870s. As in previous accounts, the poverty of the poor was associated with drink, early marriage, improvidence, irreligion, and idleness. But these were now seen as symptoms rather than causes.

Since the 1980s, neoliberal capitalism has unleashed the toxic stimulants to release the conditions, forces and relations for the demonisation of the relegated *other*.

Wacquant takes issue with Murray for his unenviable exposition of *magazine sociology* rather than theoretical and empirically rigorous academic sociology. *Punishing the poor* (Wacquant, 2009a) and *Prisons of poverty* (Wacquant, 2009b) reference Murray and his blame-allocation thesis. Wacquant also robustly responds to Wilson, Kelling, Bratton and Blair's New Labour, as well as to the location of crime within the criminal *other*. The critique of magazine sociology is that it unintelligently, uncritically and un-sociologically detaches offenders from the wider social structure. It is not because of incivilities that neighbourhoods decline, but rather because 'economic decline and persistent segregation ... feed street disorders by destabilising the local social structure and amputating the life chances of its population' (Wacquant, 2009b, p 46); it is not an innate or essentialised *otherness*, but socio-economic conditions that create the conditions for *othering*, the conditions of advanced marginality. Furthermore, it is argued that for the New Labourites after 1997, the poor, marginalised and offenders must be brought to heel by wielding the iron fist of the Leviathan state through an extended grid of penal sanctions, which contributed to the erosion of probation work (Whitehead, 2016a). In other words, the release of economic deregulation at the top end of the socio-economic hierarchy, in conjunction with an expanded penal apparatus lower down the slope of the class structure, would deal with social insecurity. Accordingly, the modernised criminal justice system engages in a triangular trade in human cargo, the three elements of which are: (1) neoliberal conditions of existence imposed from above by successive governments; (2) the consequential production of urban outcasts further down below the social hierarchy; and (3) the punitive and exclusionary response of an expanded criminal justice regime. The result is the fragmentation of what was once the social-welfare state, which intervened to protect its citizens from the worst excesses of market operations and penality (Wacquant, 2008, p 234). Probation, at its best, was a bulwark against the excessive use of punishment and prison, a bulwark to shore up rehabilitative inclusion for people who offend in order to mitigate othering.

Furthermore, in England and Wales, the spike in the prison population occurred after 1992/93, following a period of relative stability. Critical aspects of the Criminal Justice Act 1991 were unpicked by the retaliatory 1993 Act, the former intending to suppress the prison population. Between 1993 and 2012, the prison population almost doubled from 45,000 to 87,000, with a corresponding rate increase to 153 per 100,000 of the population. A higher proportion of convicted offenders were sentenced to custody and for longer (Carter, 2007), in addition to a higher rate of recall to prison. In England and Wales, black, Asian and minority ethic individuals make up 14% of the population but over 25% of the prison population (Coyle et al, 2016, p 114). If it can be empirically verified that different socio-economic groupings are not evenly represented in the composition of prison populations, this also applies to racial composition. In addition to the US, England and Wales, a disproportionate number of prisoners are from minority groups in New Zealand and Australia. The prison system since 1992/93, which incorporates Conservative and New Labour administrations, has been transformed into a 'key institution in the reformulation of social control practices' (Sim, 2009, p 128) targeted at a specific section of the population, which has exacerbated pejorative othering.

The subject under discussion can be regionalised. Beynon et al (1994) situate individuals, families and communities in their historical, politico-economic context (see also Kotzé, 2016; Temple, 2016). Human behaviour and responses must be excavated in relation to the forces and relations of changing material conditions, flight of capital and differential employment opportunities, specifically since the 1980s. Local and regional political, economic, ethical and social transformations are a consequence of global events that must be factored into an appreciation of the process and functioning of *othering*. Furthermore, Jones (2015) asserts that the media contribute to the creation of the *other* by pedalling pejorative stories of the human condition: those who scrounge off the state, the feckless, the work shy, the unemployed and benefit cheats. Also, there is the disproportionate practice of 'stop and search' by the police, particularly among young black men in North London, which has had a negative psychological impact. Jones (2015, p 148) includes a quotation from a youth community leader in Tottenham:

> You're aware that you're being "othered". You're aware that you're seen as almost like an enemy of the state. You're kind of danger, you're seen as most likely to commit crime, more likely to be unemployed, and it's more likely to be your fault.

Wilkinson and Pickett (2009) expand on inequality as a product of structural violence imposed from above. Inequality creates dysfunctional societies and the psychological need to establish a positive self-identity against the other to boost status. Creating a more equal society would lessen the psychological motivation to construct the other. Therefore, it is possible to excavate the concept of the other in what is a rich criminological and criminal justice literature. Nevertheless, this excavation of the other is not complete unless we consider two quotations. The first is from a 1930s' political and sociological novel (I have yet to find a student in my criminal justice module who has heard of this old Etonian turned 20th-century radical social commentator); the second is extracted from the penological literature:

> Fear of the mob is a superstitious fear. It is based on the idea that there is some mysterious, fundamental difference between rich and poor, as though they were two different races, like Negroes and the white man. But in reality there is no such difference. The mass of the rich and poor are differentiated by their incomes and nothing else, and the average millionaire is only the average dishwasher dressed in a new suit. Change places, and handy dandy, which is the justice, which is the thief. (Orwell, 1933, p 107)

> There is not, therefore, a criminal nature, but a *play of forces* which, according to the class to which individuals belong, will lead them to power or to prison: if born poor, today's magistrates would no doubt be in the convict ships; and the convicts, if they had been well born, would be presiding in the courts and dispensing justice. (Foucault, 1977, pp 288–9, emphasis added)

The Eriksson collection

At this point, let us return to the aforementioned Eriksson (2016) collection, in which you will be hard-pressed to find any references to those illustrations of the other recounted so far in this chapter. Nevertheless, in Chapter Two of the Eriksson collection, Simon (2016) puts Bauman's (1989) thesis to work when exploring the development of mass incarceration in the US, which includes the capacity of modern bureaucratic functioning to create the other, human rights violations, inhumanity and the cultural hegemony of race. Chapter Four of the Eriksson (2016) collection engages with the topic of 'prisons and the social production of immorality'. Eriksson (2016, p 78) correctly states that prisons do not exist in a vacuum as they reflect and reproduce the politico-economic ideology that contains and sustains them. This point can be taken further by noting that the realities of prison expansion, the punitive and exclusionary contours of criminal justice and penal policy, have been reconfigured by the neoliberal capitalist order and its Praetorian Guard of fearful competition, privatisation, and marketisation. Next, Chapter Five of the Eriksson collection by Bruhn, Nylander and Lindberg (2016) considers 'trends towards distantiation and objectification of the Other'. In fact, it is boldly stated that the decisive shift in Sweden's social-democratic welfare state to the neoliberal order of things has 'engendered a technocratic change that profoundly reifies and dehumanizes the Other – in this context the prisoner' (Bruhn et al, 2016, p 102). Finally, it is instructive to refer to Barker's (2016) Chapter Nine on 'Bauman's moral duty'. Within the contextual disciplines of criminology and sociology, 'the criminal justice system is a mass sorting machine of harms, blames and pain' (Barker, 2016, p 189). The assimilated combination of the macro-transition from the Keynesian dispensation to the neoliberal order, from the Symbolic order of social welfare and solidarity to the release of energies associated with the anti-ethical Real, and from probation, the personal social services and the supporting ideology of rehabilitation to the expansion of retributive punishment and prisons have clustered together and gathered momentum to reset politico-economic and ethico-social boundaries (on 'liquid modernity', see Bauman, 2000). This is evidenced in the reconstruction of criminal justice and penal policy towards the construction of the demonised and relegated other, indexed in the forced decline of probation services (Whitehead, 2015a, 2016a). It is my view that Eriksson and her colleagues do not go far enough from analysis to resolution, which we will return to later in the final chapter.

Intermediate summation of relegation and demonisation

So far, we have considered illustrations, explanations and manifestations of pejorative othering. We have stepped into the stream of history and referred to the 20th and 21st centuries: the Nazi death camps; the dislocated movement of refugees; and the European Union referendum. Currently, we are exploring an organisational perspective appertaining to the criminal justice system. Accordingly, the *other* is mapped out to develop what is an ascribed mark of difference that draws attention to how we behave towards each other under specific conditions of existence. Although a cogent case can be advanced to eradicate the construction of the other through a radical transformation in how we organise ourselves – this is the fundamental business of politics, economics and ethics (see Chapter Four) – my immediate preoccupation in the next chapter is more modest but no less important and urgent. We should be reminded that at the level of personal, national and international relations, including the criminal justice system and what is left of probation and also the 21 community rehabilitation companies (CRCs), an *immediate* duty to and obligation for others is a pressing consideration. Moral responsibility transcends prevailing political and economic arrangements but is always up against it, and the present situation is indubitably difficult. However, this does not mean that there is no scope to advance the content of, and argument for, the moral interest. It is self-evidently the case that current circumstances are intellectually and morally less favourable than they were, and the pathway to an alternative future is blocked with uncertainties and frustrations. The weight of history and the recent events recounted earlier press heavily upon us. This is not a favourable platform to initiate a change of direction from below. Who is interested in the ethics of criminal justice, the language of moral obligation, what happens to refugees and the vision of a united Europe or universal ethical community? It is clear that not everyone is.

It is vital to assert that evidence for the demonisation and relegation of the offending other in criminal justice has, over recent decades, been exacerbated by the same transformative forces that helped to frame the discussion in Chapter One. Specifically, the expansion of retributive punishment and prison, and the modernisation and transformation of the criminal justice system in general and probation in particular, reflect and reproduce the organisational logics of neoliberal capitalism. The process and function of othering is contingent upon specific politico-economic conditions of existence; they do not reflect essential or natural conditions of life on earth. The production and reproduction of relegation, demonisation and wasted lives are undoubtedly exacerbated when meshed with the expansion of retributive punishment and the prison establishments of the criminal justice system. Wacquant, for example, advances the thesis that neoliberalism, as the latest phase of capitalism that has solidified its globalised grip, is responsible for accruing economic benefits for the few at the expense of the many. The penal state has been expanded in the US and UK as a functional response to address the disorders of post-industrialism and the threats from urban outcasts lower down the social hierarchy. He makes it clear 'that the "upsizing" of the penal sector of the American state is causally and functionally related to the "downsizing" of its welfare sector in the post-Keynesian age' (Wacquant, 2009b, p 3). This analysis also applies to the UK. Prisons were expanded to contain supernumerary populations culled largely from the economically insecure sections of the population *and* minority ethnic groups (Coyle et al, 2016). Wacquant (2009b, p 92) summons the work of Rusche and Kirchheimer (1968 [1939]) and similar studies, which indicates a 'close and positive correlation at the societal level between the deterioration of the labour market and the rise of the population behind bars'. The argument is advanced for a strategic fit between the economic system, conditions of the labour market, political economy, class and race, and forms of punishment adopted by the state increasingly since the 1980s. It has been argued that New Labour modernisers after 1997 stigmatised, blamed and punished different groups of people labelled as *deficient subjectivities* (Tyler, 2013, p 162).

Before concluding this chapter to turn to the ethical contestation of othering, it is necessary to offer further reflections on the relationship between crime and punishment, the criminal justice system, the neoliberal capitalist order of things, and the reproduction of the exclusionary other. Ascribing salience to neoliberalism does not mean it constitutes *a theory of everything*, but it must be taken seriously when excavating profound transformations in criminal justice, probation and penal policy imposed during the last 20 years by the political class. Since the late 1970s, neoliberalism has been selected as the politico-economic order of choice in England and Wales and the US (on its uneven development in other countries, see Harvey, 2005; on neoliberal convergence, see Peters, 2012). It has acquired a beguiling orthodoxy; the slightest whiff of an alternative world view is quickly relegated to the laughably quirky or dangerous – look at how the Corbyn factor, for example, is framed in the media. It is contoured by a distinctive configuration of mental conceptions (Harvey, 2010) that have ideologically and materially combined to displace the post-war Keynesian social-democratic settlement (Whitehead and Crawshaw, 2014). Its results are manifested in the reconstruction of state responsibilities and functioning, organisational reconfigurations, and human subjectivity (Hall, 2012). This galloping process that transformed the nation-state into the market-state has empirically verifiable consequences for the criminal justice system and its response to offenders. Accordingly, transformations in criminal justice in England and Wales and the US can be explained by foregrounding the significance of neoliberal political economy (the Marxist base–superstructure model constitutes a broad operating and explanatory framework), but with nuanced qualifications. It can be argued that the neoliberal order has reconfigured criminal justice to such an extent that it has splintered into a moral void to the detriment of criminal *and* social justice. This is clearly indexed in the erosion of the probation system by a thousand ideological and material cuts. Neoliberalism, which elevates the primacy of economics over ethics, has *de-moralised* the system by advancing the punitive exclusion and bureaucratic management of troublesome populations. As Kotzé (2016, p 230) unhesitatingly states in his doctoral thesis, the 'reality' constructed since the 1980s by neoliberal capitalism is a criminogenic milieu 'geared more towards stimulating rather than attenuating the worst excesses of capitalism'. This system urgently requires *re-moralisation* in order to transform the conditions of human existence. We will pick this up in the final chapter.

Selective literature review on neoliberalism, crime, punishment and criminal justice

Reiner (2007) advances the empirically grounded proposition that the rise in crime, followed by a discernible shift in the direction of law-and-order punitive responses, can be explained by neoliberal political economy. We know that criminal statistics are contentiously inaccurate, but there is agreement on a rapid increase in recorded crime from the 1950s to the 1980s, a crime explosion from the 1980s to 1992, followed by a crime decline after 1992 (Reiner, 2007, p 64; but see Kotzé [2016], who modifies the 'crime decline' thesis). This pattern broadly continues today as there were 6.8 million incidents of crime in England and Wales during the year ending in March 2015. This was 7% down on the previous year and the lowest estimate since 1981. According to this statistical review, there has been a steady decline in property crime since the mid-1990s, specifically vehicle theft and burglary. The decline in 'conventional' crime is also supported by the International Crime Victims Survey (ICVS) due to reflexive securitisation. This statistical grit causes aggravation to the general thesis that neoliberalism means more crime, but we should not be too hasty in our assessment. While it does appear that certain conventional crimes have declined, and that there is the possibility of mutation and obsolescence, it is important to draw attention to the components of an alternative thesis:

- there are methodological problems associated with the scope and accuracy of the ICVS; and
- neoliberal globalisation has generated new opportunities for 'unconventional' crimes and harms in response to changes in market conditions – online trade in counterfeit pharmaceuticals, human trafficking, cybercrime, diverse opportunities afforded by the Internet and bullying at school and the workplace.

Reiner (2007, p 107) digs deeper by asserting that neoliberalism 'is associated with greater inequality, long-term unemployment, and social exclusion'. He also identifies tougher criminal justice and penal attitudes by recourse to Durkheim and Merton on anomie and the release of egoistic individualism. In other words, anomie weakens the symbolic efficiency of socio-moral controls, energises egoism and stimulates competition on a structural platform of capitalist exchange relations. Moreover, neoliberalism displaced Keynesian conventions to establish conditions of existence that transformed the discourse on crime and criminal justice. In doing so, it weakened 'the levers available to governments to regulate the economic and social divisions, exclusion and injustice that are the root causes of crime' (Reiner, 2007, p 153). Notwithstanding the problems associated with the crime decline thesis, and challenges to this position, Reiner asserts that the crime explosion of the 1980s was caused by ethical and social damage inflicted by the neoliberal tsunami. This created the conditions for long-term unemployment, poverty and inequality, the central analytical and explanatory factors pertinent for theorising the other.

Bell (2011) addresses the same nexus of variables. Located within a neoliberal excavation of globalisation, the production of exaggerated risks, the features of late-modernity, elongated social hierarchy (the growing gap between rich and poor) and intolerance, Bell pursues the discussion on structural conditions, crime and criminal justice. The argument advanced is that there is no automatic relationship between neoliberalism and harsher forms of criminal justice and penal policy. However, neoliberalism's ideological features, structural conditions and economic priorities create the conditions that are *more likely* than not to produce more punitive responses. In other words, egoistic individualism meshes with the state's demand for enhanced levels of responsibility to justify punishment that complements the approach of neoclassical criminology. This configuration of interests neutralises the state's moral responsibility for the socio-economic conditions of offenders: it is your fault, a result of your own bad choices, so why should we do anything about it? Frankly, you have failed to take advantage of the new opportunities that we have provided.

Garland (2001) enriches the analysis when propounding that the late-modern crime complex since the 1970s, mainly in the US and

UK, has responded to the predicament posed by an increased sense of insecurity and risk, including rising crime during the 1980s, in three ways: *adaptation*, *denial* and *acting out*. In fact, contemporary crime control policies operate at two distinct levels: instrumental means-to-an-end; and expressive-emotional communication of cogent messages throughout the social body. The latter, resonating with retributive punishment, condemnation, denunciation and repudiation, has emerged as an identifiable feature of populist penal politics. In the trilogy *Punishment and welfare* (Garland, 1985), *Punishment and modern society* (Garland, 1990) and *The culture of control* (Garland, 2001), Garland advances a theory of historical-social change with implications for penal policy and the operational functioning of criminal justice. Beginning in the 1985 text with an analysis of mid- to late Victorian penality, underpinned by an ideology replete with individualism and a laissez-faire minimalist state, Garland tracks the emergence of the *penal-welfare* complex during the early years of the 20th century. Specifically, when excavating the system of penality during the 19th century, and then the contours of penal-welfare from the 1900s to the 1970s, concluding with transformative developments since the 1980s, it is elucidated that institutions of criminal justice have their own internal dynamics and contain the scope to develop according to internal professional logics, values and institutional responsibilities. However, criminal justice is also a *state-directed practice* implicated in the management of disorderly behaviours whose practices are shaped by wider social movements located within the constraints of macro-social structures. Garland's thesis utilises the Marxist base–superstructure model, yet without obsessive devotion to one theoretical position. In fact, he draws theoretical inspiration from Durkheim, Weber and Foucault, as well as Marx (1990), in the explication of how penal policies and criminal justice practices emerge, develop and change over time under different historico-structural conditions.

The 2001 text advances the argument that it is not intellectually feasible to explain contemporary crime control strategies in isolation from wider macro-level political, socio-economic and cultural variables. A central point is that the late-modern crime complex is not solely a response to rising crime rates – allegedly falling in the US and UK over recent years. Rather, it is an adaptive response to late-modern conditions and the preoccupation with crime and associated insecurities, the declining efficacy of rehabilitation, and a less generous attitude towards an inclusivist social-welfare state. Consequently, there is a strategic 'fit' between penal arrangements, the contours of the criminal justice system and transformational responses, macro-structural factors, ideology, hegemony, class relations and the authoritarian musculature of power arrogated by the state to respond to those problems that *its policies have exacerbated rather than ameliorated*. The conditions of existence and surface of emergence for the late-modern criminal justice complex, which includes the modernised and culturally transformed probation system (Whitehead, 2015a, 2016a), is the 'risky, insecure character of today's social and economic relations' (Garland, 2001, p 194). This complex is more preoccupied with risk, harm, dangerous predators, rigorous mechanisms of control, maintaining order and public protection. The roots for these transformation contours lie deep within the socio-economic dislocations of the 1970s and what we can describe as the neoliberal turn.

Cavadino and Dignan (2006) endorse the association between crime, criminal justice, penal policy and neoliberal capitalism, or between punishment and the labour market alluded to earlier in Rusche and Kirchheimer (1968 [1939]). Credence is given to the juxtaposition of neoliberal politico-economy, the fight against crime, zero tolerance, punishment in the community, prison inflation, tougher enforcement practices, longer sentences and an abundance of legislation. However, Cavadino and Dignan (2006, p 12) hitch themselves to a 'radical pluralist analytical framework', similar to Garland (1990). This position slips through the net of neoliberalism as a *theory of everything*, being not a rigid application of Marxist theory, but a pluralist model that meshes ideology with material *and* cultural components. Cavadino and Dignan acknowledge critical political and economic, ethical and cultural, turning points under Nixon, Reagan, Clinton and Bush in the US, as well as Thatcher, Major and Blair in the UK. They advance empirical evidence to support the link between state formation and transformations in penality: neoliberal countries; conservative corporatist welfare states; social-democratic corporatism; and the oriental corporatist state. Cavadino and Dignan (2006) explicate linkages between the neoliberal platform and penal expansion.

Wacquant (2008, 2009a, 2009b) has constructed an impressive body of work. To repeat, he refers to Rusche and Kirchheimer (Wacquant, 2009b, p 92) and other studies that support a positive correlation between the structural conditions of the labour market and forms of punishment. There is no direct statistical link between crime rates and incarceration rates. However, from Thatcher, to Major, to Blair after 1997, the penalisation of poverty is the:

> indispensable functional complement to the imposition of precarious and underpaid wage labour and to the draconian reduction in social protection that the New Labourites have made the touchstone of the Third Way between capitalism and social democracy. Economic deregulation and penal overregulation go hand in hand. (Wacquant, 2009b, p 120)

Additionally, 'the surge and exaltation of the police, courts, and prisons in First and Second World societies over the past two decades are integral to the neoliberal revolution' (Wacquant, 2009b, p 171). Wacquant establishes the instrumental, functional, expressive and symbolic (borrowing from Marx and Durkheim) linkages between the imposition of the neoliberal order, the spread of social disorder, the reproduction of urban outcasts (Wacquant, 2008) and marginality, culminating in governments formulating the judgement to select harsher criminal justice and penal responses towards the urban poor. The Leviathan state has pursued a policy of criminal justice and penal expansionism through incarceration, related to the decline in the assistantial welfare state, and coupled with an inflated *bureaucratic field* to manage, contain, control, punish and exclude behavioural disorders produced under neoliberal conditions. Economic violence imposed from above in the form of deindustrialisation, unemployment, flexible wage labour, social insecurity, despair and the truncation of life chances are functionally related to changing responses from within the criminal justice system, which includes the relegation and demonisation of the other.

Rodger's (2008) analysis resonates with Wacquant on the erosion of social welfare, transformations in social policy and the implications for crime, criminal justice and penal policy that merge to reconstruct a harsher response to problem populations under conditions of late-modernity. Rodger, like Wacquant, makes a strong case for the state's criminalisation and penalisation of poverty and inequality. Next, Leys (2003, p 74) comments that while:

> Blair had promised that Labour would be 'tough on crime and tough on the causes of crime', it was easier to be the former than the latter, and more in tune with his emphasis on making individuals responsible for their actions no matter what the circumstances.

Finally, Wilkinson and Pickett (2009) state that inequality, exacerbated by the neoliberal turn, is having an adverse effect on health, physical and mental well-being, education, and welfare, as well as producing a harsher penal system. Accordingly, the importance of foregrounding the impact of neoliberalism cannot be avoided. This discussion enriches excavating the demonised, relegated and excluded other, as well as the process and function of pejorative othering.

If we turn from excavating the nexus of linkages to explanation, Bell (2011) does not prosecute some deterministic proposition. Rather, she accommodates ambiguity instead of certainty. Garland (1990) and Cavadino and Dignan (2006) construct a pluralistic model that allows for competing explanations. Wacquant foregrounds Marx *and* Durkheim, the operatic duet of the instrumental and expressive, while ascribing explanatory efficacy to the instrumental impacts of neoliberalism and its effects on behaviour (subjectivity), criminal justice policies and the Leviathan's penal practices. Rodger (2008), in conjunction with Bell (2011), argue against a rigid determinism that unambiguously links the nexus of variables. There is no unambiguous algebraic equation where A = neoliberalism produces B = crime. Wilkinson and Pickett (2009) support the thesis that the neoliberal platform damages the ethical fabric of society by creating an elongated hierarchy between economic elites and the rest (see the earlier reference to distantiation). The widening gap between the apex and base of the pyramid erodes trust and respect between those peering down and those gazing up. It is the politically manufactured distance that releases the energy to create, punish and exclude the relegated *other*, rather than enhance mutual understanding and coexistence. There is a broad consensus of opinion that neoliberalism established, and continues to sustain, politico-economic conditions with implications for criminal behaviour, punishment and criminal justice (see discussion in Kotzé, 2016; Temple, 2016). The distinctive features of neoliberal ideology, structural-material transformations and ethico-cultural decline have culminated in a retreat from solidaristic experience (compare New Labour penal politics since 1997 with the tenor of old Labour's *review* in Home Office, 1977). Neoliberalism promotes a way of doing things that reserves an active role for the state as the promoter of 'market solutions and facilitator of competition between rational, free thinking individuals' (Bell, 2011, p 140). Moreover, the neoliberal revolution constitutes a 'political project to re-establish the conditions for capital accumulation and to restore the power of economic elites' (Harvey, 2005, p 19), which, for Žižek (1992), has aggressively jettisoned the *Symbolic* into the *Real* – just look at the spectacular collapse of probation and social work with offenders (Whitehead, 2015a, 2016a). However, there are nuanced qualifications lurking at the edges of the neoliberal hypothesis. In fact, these nuanced qualifications stray into the territory of Cavadino and Dignan (2006) and Garland (1990) to support a radical pluralist analytical framework.

We can summarise this discussion as follows: the ideological and material reconstruction of the criminal justice system in general, and probation in particular, which culminated in the creation of 21 CRCs in October 2014, put the focus on the act rather than actor, the deed not the person in their socio-economic context. The accompanying narrative of just deserts, retributive punishment, exclusionary prison, administrative and bureaucratic efficiency, and the rational-calculator model of offending has de-*moral*ised and, in turn, dehumanised the system of criminal and social justice. The power to punish has reconstructed a morally impoverished criminal justice system, indexed by probation's demise, and the 'loss of interest in people in both theoretical and policy domains' (Hudson, 1993, p 63) is disturbing. Furthermore, discriminatory practices appertaining to class, gender and race, the economics of inequality, and the imposition of punishment directed towards economically disadvantaged groups has exacerbated the problem of pejorative othering. In other words, 'at every stage of the economic cycle, it is mainly the poor, the unemployed and the minority populations who are the most heavily penalised' (Hudson, 1993, p 72). This brings us full circle to Wacquant's thesis: neoliberal capitalism has spawned urban outcasts, expelled from the post-war settlement solidarity project, and, in turn, the criminal justice system has been functionally reconfigured, or *modernised*, to contain but also reproduce the demonised and relegated other. Wacquant's triangular realignment of state–market–citizen under neoliberal operating conditions and the expansion of punitive confinement constitute a double negation of othering – first, the neoliberal order and, second, the modernised criminal justice system. This is a mess of our own making and reflects the hollowing out of ethical considerations and moral responses. It may well be possible to advance different explanations of othering, as alluded to earlier, but we cannot avoid the conditions of existence imposed by neoliberalism and its exclusionary effects.

The next chapter raids a number of resources and academic disciplines to contest the process and function of pejorative othering *whatever its determinate causes*. These resources and disciplines respond to the stream of history illustrated in Chapter One, and contest the neoliberal reconstruction of criminal justice and penal policy explored in Chapter Two. I want to raise the profile of some lesser-known resources to confront the reproduction of the demonised and relegated other in all its forms. Again, the charge could be laid of a lack of balance, but I must of necessity be selective in my use of resources in a book of this length and scope in order to illustrate the moral contestation of othering. After completing the next task, a resolution to the problem will be advanced in the final chapter.

THREE

Contesting the other:
sinking ethical shafts

The question threading its unsettling course through the Western philosophical tradition since the era of classical Greece, several centuries after the Agricultural Revolution, is: *why is there something rather than nothing?* There is no essential requirement for the existence of something rather than nothing, no necessity for planet earth and its universe of orbiting satellites, not even the existential necessity for Homo sapiens appearing 200,000 years ago. Theological perspectives, religious sensibilities and assorted wishful thinkers are disturbed by the thought of a series of inexplicable accidents that began with a big bang 4.5 billion years ago. Surely, the fact that there is something rather than nothing is for a reason. For example, this *something* is infused with purpose because human beings exist for the pleasure of the divine presence. There may well be one or two glitches along the way – a massacre here, a mass shooting there, pogroms directed against Jews, chemical attacks, racial tensions, the periodic slaughter of innocents, cultural revolutions, the hideous obscenities of the Syrian and other conflicts, and assorted genocides. However, we are invited to take comfort in the thought that God, or the Absolute, Reason or Spirit, is up there and out there bringing a transcendent purpose to fruition through the historical process by establishing a foothold in human consciousness. History may well be a slaughter bench; the bones of the innocent bleached white by the centuries. However, do not despair because, eventually, all will be well. What webs we weave with fragile strands of myth and imaginary scripts to dispel despair and cling to the kingdom of hope.

Given that there is something of which we are a part, rather than nothing, a silence, an absence, though we cannot say how or why with certainty, a subsidiary question of equal importance is why the history of *this* something has not assumed the content and form of something else? Since the Agricultural Revolution around 12,000 years ago (see Chapter One), why this account of human existence and not another? Why have things turned out as they have, and not differently? We could be recounting a very different human story, one of ethical triumphs, mass cooperation networks, national and international mutual coexistence, and living as one humanity under conditions of equality within the circuits of a moral economy. We could even be recounting a very different history of politico-economic systems, probation, criminal justice and penal policy to that which has been imposed from above by our political grandmasters and their coterie of special advisors (Whitehead, 2016a). Since the 1980s, they have compiled spreadsheets of unit costs and obsess about effectiveness and efficiency, but they have little appreciation of historical worth or traditional value. Having made these observations, posed our questions and engaged in the intriguing spectacle of counterfactuals (what has not happened but could have under different conditions, based on different judgements and decisions), I turn directly in this chapter to the ethical contestation of othering. Desires, drives and our relations with others are framed by social structures that, in turn, create the conditions of existence that provoke ethical questions. The more the social structure facilitates the separation of one from another, the greater the opportunity to fashion the demonised and relegated other. In the interests of the well-being of all, this state of affairs must be contested and transcended. This is the purpose of the current chapter and resources are available to achieve this task.

The current chapter explores a number of ethical perspectives, gleaned from a cloud of witnesses who have been summonsed to give evidence, not before a magistrates' or crown court, but before the slaughter bench of history. Whether we like it or not, we are constantly confronted with the demands of duty, the rigorous claim of moral obligation towards the other. Most of us do not exist or choose to exist in solitary confinement. We do not want to emulate Descartes huddled around a stove in winter to keep warm, in splendid isolation, whether thinking great thoughts or not. At some point, we leave the closeted confinement of our own minds to step outside of ourselves, where we intersect with others. How are we going to do this during the early decades of the 21st century, and what form should it take? Self-evidently it is much easier to pose the question than answer it, but the demands of duty and obligation towards each other persist regardless of attendant difficulties. The benefit of inviting you, the reader, to attend court is to facilitate the formulation of judgement and the burden of decision-making, in other words, to rethink the contours of duty and obligation towards each other. Fundamentally, how are we going to live alongside and act towards each other in order to avoid reproducing the process and function of pejorative othering? This is the central question being hurled in our direction.

Therefore, you are being invited in this chapter to hear and weigh some of the evidence to make up your own mind on pressing matters presented in Chapters One and Two. It should be clarified that this is only part of the evidence, not an exhaustive list of witnesses or written testimony. Nevertheless, different positions and intellectual traditions are represented – theological and philosophical, ethical, personalist and existentialist, literary allusions, biblical references, and psychoanalytical insights. It includes testimony as diverse as Homer, Old Testament resources from the 8th-century BCE and letters written in Greek, before stepping into the 20th century. Importantly – reader take note – some of the evidence incorporates witness testimony *presented in the first person* to accentuate its dramatic effect, conflated with other evidence in the form of written submissions. Although adopting this unusual stylistic method (sometimes we have to try something different), I remain faithful to the original sources. The invitation is to imagine that you are an interested observer in the public gallery, or even a juror sworn in by the presiding judge. Once the evidence has been presented, listened to and judiciously evaluated, you will be confronted with making a decision. I need to warn you that based upon the assimilation of this evidence, I will be arguing for transformative ethical and political action in Chapter Four in order to move beyond the orthodox consensus. In other words, I will proceed from the many disturbing illustrations of othering considered earlier, its multiple causes and manifestations, to establish a different platform for our mutual coexistence. You, of course, must make up your own mind on these matters, but all our futures depend on the decisions that we collectively make. Let us begin by hearing the evidence of someone who racked up four doctorates in philosophy, theology, music and medicine. He was the first to step into the witness box and eminently qualified to do so. Let us allow him to speak for himself.

Call Albert Schweitzer into the witness box

Before proceeding with my personal testimony, I confirm to the court that the following identifiers constitute my life's work. There are volumes of autobiography (Schweitzer, 1955, 1962) in addition to Parts 1 and 2 of *The philosophy of civilization* (Schweitzer, 1929, 1961). There is also a copious secondary literature by Seaver (1947), Mozley (1950) and Russell (1941). It may also be of interest to consult an informative documentary if you are approaching my life and work for the first time (available at: www.youtube.com/watch?v=Gf4B9vOsOCY).

In the Preface to Part 2 of my *Philosophy of civilisation* (Schweitzer, 1929), I asserted that the fundamental content and meaning of ethics is *reverence for life*. What is good consists in maintaining, promoting and enhancing human life; destroying, injuring and limiting life are evil. This text subjected the history of ethical systems to the criterion of reverence for life that began with

Socrates, Plato, Aristotle and other contributions from the classical world. I proceeded to incorporate religious and philosophical world views that have appeared over the centuries: the pre- and post-Renaissance perspectives of Hartley, Hobbes, Locke, Bentham, Smith, Hutcheson and Shaftesbury; and the Enlightenment, with Kant, Hegel, Schopenhauer and Nietzsche. All these ethical systems are exposed to rigorous critique before explaining what I mean by reverence for life, its civilising power and mission to all the peoples of the world. Writing in the period after the catastrophic events of the First World War, I diagnosed, but also lamented, what I think is fundamentally wrong with the human condition. Therefore, my evidence is that we must attend to material, cultural *and* spiritual development to cultivate ourselves beyond the vacuity of stupid entertainment and the constant imperative to enjoy. We should take time to read books in order to enrich our minds and learn how to act in the world because we have lost a sense of higher ideals, which came crashing down at Flanders. Since the 19th century, mass culture and relentless work schedules have reduced human beings to cogs in a vast industrial and bureaucratic machine that is out of control and that has eroded creative artistry. Like Weber, my fellow German, I see threats directed towards humanity from modernity, scientific technology and a scheming and calculating attitude, and technical rationality has swamped the appeal of substantive rationality (the calculating attitude before values). The European continent has witnessed a declining code of manners that does not support a progressive civilisation thesis. In fact, there has been a coarsening of sensibilities manifested in indifference to other people that European centres of power encouraged leading up to and during the First World War.

I lamented that post-First World War social conditions eroded ascribing to all peoples human value and dignity. This is because many sections of the human race have become merely raw material and property in human form. We stopped thinking about and striving for what it means to be human. There was a lack of reasoned application to ethics, and it is ethical enquiry that strikes to the nature and progress of human civilisation and to the formation of human subjectivity. The material, scientific, positivist and technical contours of existence have eclipsed the ethical and the spiritual, which create the conditions and release the forces to construct the relegated and demonised other. We have lost a sense of history and heritage, both national and European, and there are dangers inherent in raw populist nationalism, which has the capacity to distort how we relate to each other in a way that transcends the exchange relation and profit motive. However, let me try to offer something positive by proceeding from analysis and lament to restoration, predicated on directing attention towards ethics. Also, to reflect on and action politico-economic arrangements to facilitate better human relations and the ideals of justice, and prevent damage to the neighbour, which urgently requires a new world view that I distil in the ethic of reverence for life. It must assert and value life in and of itself, put people first, attend to the well-being of all to contest and reduce the anti-ethic of othering. To survive as a species, we must put universalism before particularism.

I must return my evidence to *Civilisation and ethics* (Schweitzer, 1929). In this book, I reflected, as alluded to earlier, on a number of philosophical, religious and ethical perspectives and maintained the position that the salient gift of Christianity to the world is that the ethical is constituted in the individual's active self-devotion towards others, in other words, the other as neighbour, not disposable enemy. The anti-ethic of liberal capitalism extracts more than it gives when endorsing that it is more blessed to receive than to give. The Judaeo-Christian ethic is the opposite because it is premised on sacrificial giving more than receiving. Accordingly, it is not possible to live life to the full at the expense of others and by engaging in pejorative othering. The evidence I lay before this court can be condensed in the following working definition:

The basic principle of ethics, that principle which is a necessity of thought, which has a definite content, which is ever bringing itself into steady, living, and practical agreement with reality, proclaims itself to be: Devotion to life out of reverence for life. (Schweitzer, 1929, p 243)

This means, as a basic matter of practical reason, that assisting rather than relegating and demonising the other is nothing less than a sacred duty. Human life may well be a freakish evolutionary accident, but we must take steps to do all we can to facilitate human welfare, adopt a stance towards the other person that transcends negative othering and practise self-renunciation, not aggrandisement at the expense of the other. You can, if you want to, gain the whole world, but this could be at the expense of your soul, of your potential for humanity. Whoever shall lose his life shall find it and save it, which is consistent with my ethic and philosophy of reverence for life. Othering must be contested and transcended in an ethical philosophy of reverence for life that has universal applicability.

When Albert Schweitzer stood down from the witness box, the clerk of the court read the following supportive statement to the jurors and public gallery.

The witness testimony of Dr Schweitzer we have just heard elucidates that reverence for life does not pretend to certain knowledge of the world or what the history of the world may mean. It does not formulate a world view in the style of the philosophers of history, but rather advances a life view. Reverence for life is constitutive not of speculative reason, but of practical reason that affirms the sacredness of existence, which is universal in its demand and scope. Consequently, Dr Schweitzer issues an ethically inspired practical invitation to:

> Find yourselves some secondary work, an inconspicuous one,
> perhaps a secret one. Open your eyes and look for a human
> being or some work devoted to human welfare which needs
> from someone a little time or friendliness, a little sympathy,
> or sociability, or work. (Schweitzer, 1929, p 260)

Furthermore, Dr Schweitzer does not advance an ethico-cultural
critique of 19th-century liberal capitalism throughout his ethical
enquiries, nor does he address directly the concept of the pejorative
other even though it is implied. Nevertheless, he does tangentially
analyse its effects when issuing the summons for the restoration of
ethical responsibility that affirms life per se, which has implications
for politico-economic structures, in addition to the rationale and
functioning of people-facing organisations including the criminal
justice system. In fact, he rigorously questions how it is possible to
attain the standard of economic justice and, by implication, social
justice unless it is premised upon the morality of reverence for life
(Schweitzer, 1929, p 277).

Many contemporary politicians continue to miss the point in their
politico-economic musings because they all too often reduce the
dictum of being 'better off' to a fiscal rather than moral calculator.
Even after the calamitous crisis of capitalism of 2007/08, in addition
to a change of government leadership in the UK in July 2016
following the European Union vote, the country remains confronted
with the urgent requirement of how to organise itself morally. This
is as urgent now as when Schweitzer was writing decades ago,
not only because of the anti-ethical tendencies of the neoliberal
capitalist order, but also because of the amoral and de-moralising
transformations in criminal justice (and other organisations)
addressed in the previous chapter that, at the organisational level,
reflect and reproduce the dominant political and economic system.
If Schweitzer were alive today, it is intriguing to ponder that he
would be in the vanguard of demanding, for example, the restoration
of probation as a social work organisation in order to contest the

denigration of the other that has occurred through a vastly expanded prison system.

_____

Call Dietrich Bonhoeffer into the witness box

Before proceeding with my personal testimony, I confirm to the court that the following identifiers constitute my own work as an expert witness before this court. Some of my primary texts can be found in Bonhoeffer (1955, 1963, 1966, 1971). Secondary texts include Bethge (1970), Dumas (1971) and Metaxas (2010), whose text complements the documentary cinematic presentation of my life, 'Agent of grace'.

I would like to provide some evidence to this court that appeared in the book published as *Letters and papers from prison* (Bonhoeffer, 1971). These reflections can be traced to the period of July 1944 to February 1945, which was an extremely difficult time because I was in prison in my own country of Germany during the Second World War under the Nazi regime. While in prison, I sketched an outline for a book that subsequently came to the attention of my good friend Eberhard Bethge. This book would have been no more than 100 pages and divided into three thematically related chapters:

1. A stocktaking of Christianity.
2. The real meaning of the Christian faith.
3. Conclusions.

My testimony before this court may well be interpreted as irregular and unorthodox when I say that a person's relationship with God does not mean religious contact to the highest, most powerful and best Being that it is possible to imagine. This is a mistaken view of transcendence and questionable use of language as there is no Being up there or out there, literally speaking. This naive world view should have been jettisoned at the scientific Renaissance with Copernicus,

Galileo and Kepler. Instead, this theological-mythical language of a relationship with a transcendent God is not about metaphysics, but rather about existing for others, so it is vital to reorder our thinking. It is about life on earth and how it should be ordered and conducted, not orientation towards the heavens. In other words, existing for others constitutes the new life. The transcendental does not amount to infinite and unattainable doctrinal tasks, but means turning to the neighbour who needs me here and now and who stands within reach in any given situation. Think about the new model of human existence signified not by the insatiable desires, drives and relentless demands of consumerism and its accompanying status symbols, but by a cross that presents a radical existential challenge to lives immersed in self-interest. Be men and women for others rather than pursue self-aggrandisement at the expense of the other. This is what it means to be human and the true meaning of religion. What is more, the Church is only and can only be the Church when it exists for others. It should sell off its accumulated earthly treasures and put the Vatican up for sale, and protestant denominations should follow this example to improve the lot of the poorest members of society. If we can reorient our lives and the organisation of the Church according to this model of existence, then we would follow in the footsteps of the one who was the definitive man for others. Accordingly, I want to achieve the re-conceptualisation of our understanding of religion in general, and Christianity in particular. I think the essence of the Christian faith that Schweitzer understands as devotion to others can be similarly defined from a theological perspective:

Encounter with Jesus Christ is the key to man's understanding of God, of a transcendent life and of the spiritual. This encounter must first be seen as an orientation of the human life in the experience of Jesus as the man for others. (Bonhoeffer, 1973, p 15)

This is what I stated in the book published as *True patriotism* (1973). I am talking about a new humanity that is freedom from anxieties about the self, rather than some special relationship with a higher being, as the sole ground of human existence. This is the new master signifier for life on earth.

When Dietrich Bonhoeffer left the witness box, the clerk of the court read the following supportive statement to the assembled jurors and those in the public gallery.

Dr Bonhoeffer's testimony should be located within the broader context of his family and the German nation during the Second World War, professional life and pastoral and academic work. He was born in Breslau on 4 February 1906. In 1928, he spent a year in Barcelona as an assistant pastor to a German-speaking Lutheran congregation, where 'He would see how the so-called other half lived, meeting and spending time with people whose businesses had failed, with victims of poverty and crime, and with truly desperate individuals, as well as with bona fide criminals' (Metaxas, 2010, p 78). In 1940, after the start of the Second World War, Bonhoeffer joined the *Abwehr*, which provided a cover for resistance work. He also continued to work at his book on *Ethics* (Bonhoeffer, 1955). He was involved in Operation 7 to save a number of Jews, and by February 1942, was being watched by the Gestapo. He was subsequently arrested on 5 April 1943 and his next 18 months were spent at Tegel prison. At this time, the Nazis were not aware of his involvement in a conspiracy to kill Hitler. His circumstances deteriorated after the failed Stauffenberg bomb plot in July 1944 that implicated Bonhoeffer, and on 8 October 1944, he was removed from Tegel and taken to the Gestapo prison at Prinz-Albrecht Strasse. On 7 February 1945, he was transferred to Buchenwald concentration camp, where he spent the next seven weeks. Finally, he was transferred from Buchenwald to Flossenburg before being tried and executed at dawn on 9 April 1945, a few days before the end of the war.

Dr Bonhoeffer's theology and Christology is rooted in the Pauline (this is the Apostle Paul's) understanding of justice and equality, the expression of responsible action to and for *others* in a world come of age, that is, a world situated beyond the Renaissance and Enlightenment, and informed by successive scientific revolutions. Dumas (1971, p 139) believes that Bonhoeffer considered *Ethics* (Bonhoeffer, 1955) his magnum opus, in which he argued that the reality of God revealed in Jesus of Nazareth is the starting point for Christian ethics. Accordingly, the ethical demand calls for 'the complete surrender of one's own life to the other man. Only the selfless man lives responsibly, and this means that only the selfless man *lives*' (Bonhoeffer, 1955, p 225, emphasis in original). This takes us from the process and designation of othering to a new mental conception of the self and the other that begins with an act of self-sacrifice. This ethic opposes egoism and the pathway advocated by Nietzsche's (1844–1900) *Übermensch*, who inverts Christian morality beyond the proclamation of the 'death of God' by trampling over others with disdain. Dr Bonhoeffer agrees with Dr Schweitzer that this has implications for our understanding of human existence, the sense we have of self and our cognitive-emotional engagement with others, as well as the judgements we formulate and decisions we make about how we organise ourselves alongside each other in the city. To repeat, the Church can only legitimately claim to be the Church when it turns outward to exist for others, not inward to engage in convoluted doctrinal dances that are increasingly irrelevant to most of us on the outside looking in. This is the meaning and manifestation of *agapē* (or love).

According to Dr Bonhoeffer, participation in the sufferings of God in the midst of the world is more than an ethical response of solidarity with the weak, poor and excluded. It is, as he theologically expressed it in *Ethics*, 'participation in the indivisible whole of the divine reality' (Dumas, 1971, p 191). This theological and anthropological position asserts that true freedom can only be found in turning towards the neighbour in a basic act of moral and social solidarity and equality, not the pursuit of stupid and ephemeral pleasures as the acme of indulgent self-interest at the expense of others:

not self-aggrandisement, but self-renunciation; not involvement in relegating or demonising others to enhance the self or to stake out territorial identity, but self-sacrifice for the other as an act of mature and responsible humanity; not particularism, but universalism. As stated towards the end of his life in *Letters and papers from prison* (during 1943–44):

> Consequently the Christian is called to follow the reality of Jesus Christ in his godforsakeness in the midst of the world come of age, so that the world can be 're-structured' – a word preferable to the religiously coloured word 'saved'. (Dumas, 1971, p 197)

The world is 're-structured' and we establish our ability to be human when we lose ourselves in the service of others, an act of mutual recognition, not finding and advancing ourselves at the expense of the other. It is disturbing to note that Schweitzer's ethic of reverence for life was systematically rejected by the Nazi state, whose anti-ethic was violently expressed in the ideology of blood, stock and race that culminated in the camps, as we saw earlier.

Call Hans Küng into the witness box

My witness testimony before this court is a summary of some work I completed in the 1970s, and it largely supports the testimony of Dr Schweitzer and Dr Bonhoeffer. I should explain that my book, *On being a Christian* (Küng, 1977), was written as an academic though accessible text on theology and Christology, with implications for theorising the moral and stimulating thinking about the other. I advanced the position, repeated now before this court, that Jesus of Nazareth (Bonhoeffer's *man for others*) is the definitive expression of God's cause in the world, the anthropological exemplar who stands at the head of a restructured humanity. This court has already heard from Dr Schweitzer, who believes that the gift bestowed by

Christianity is an ethic of self-renunciation to benefit others, and I agree with this position. It has also heard from Dr Bonhoeffer, who would agree that Jesus of Nazareth is the criterion of what it means to be human and to live humanely, even though we must also respect and learn from other world religions. We might harbour and express many different concepts of God, increasingly so since the disturbing incursions of 'death of God' theologies in the 1960s that rattled a number of us. However, I think the three of us would agree that there is one historical exemplar who represents what can accurately be described as a 'Wholly new approach to life, at an awareness transformed from the roots upward, a new basic attitude, a different scale of values, a radical rethinking and returning of the whole man' (Küng, 1977, p 546). It is this wholly new approach to life that critically questions and radically contests the relegation and demonisation of others.

At this point in the proceedings the court adjourned, but not before the clerk summarised the moral contestation of othering in the evidence of Schweitzer, Bonhoeffer and Küng. Furthermore, and more broadly, it was noted that the prophetic literature on social justice in the Old Testament canon (Jones, 1968; on the relevance for criminal justice, see also Whitehead, 2016a, ch 3), the ethical injunction to individual and community responsibility, and the new covenant of neighbourliness and love extended to enemies (see the 'Ethical Lists' in Metzger and Coogan, 1993, p 201) constitute a rich inheritance that offer a resource for ethical and anthropological reflection that responds to the *other* as neighbour rather than disposable enemy. When the proceedings resumed, it was a propitious moment to summon Dr Anderson (1988) to expand on the Old Testament canon that provides further resources for the contestation of the pejorative other.

Call Bernhard Anderson into the witness box

With the court's permission, I would like to add to Dr Küng's testimony by referring to some of my own scholarship that is pertinent to thinking about and contesting the other. One of the most remarkable features of Jewish history, situated within the wider context of Middle East politics, national conflicts and imperialist adventures – Egypt, Assyria, Babylonia, Syria and Persia, located alongside the great river systems of the Nile, Tigris and Euphrates – is the theme of national and international responsibility for each other. It should be recalled that Israel was endowed with ethical responsibilities for the weak and oppressed. If the God of Israel, Yahweh, demonstrated divine love in the act of liberation from enslavement in Egypt (this is how the exodus event was religiously understood), then divine justice demonstrably took sides with the orphan, widow and resident alien. Consequently, Israel must imitate Yahweh, just as human beings were later invited to imitate the man for others, earlier clarified in the witness testimony of Dr Bonhoeffer and Dr Küng. Every member of the covenant community, whether they were high- or low-born, rich or poor, slave or free, must be accorded equality before the law (Anderson, 1988, p 383). This means that the exploitation of others to benefit the self, injustice, exchange relations and extracting fiscal interest from loans was not part of the normative code of human relations between the self and the other. Equality and solidarity in the covenant community was the mark of a theologically inspired symbolic order, articulated in the vision of One humanity. If Alexander of Macedon dreamed of One world bound together by Greek culture, there was an Old Testament and New Testament vision of One humanity constituted by an entirely different ethico-political order of existence. Israel, at certain points in its history, contested the ethico-cultural, political and social composition of other nations in the Fertile Crescent. Israel could have been a light to these nations, just as the new covenant offered a model of a restructured humanity where the master signifier was represented by a cross rather than a sword.

The testimony of Dr Anderson was supplemented by the following addition to the proceedings, which reaches back many centuries.

> Amos, Hosea, Isaiah and Micah were Old Testament ethical prophets preoccupied with right and fair dealings between human beings. Specifically Amos, during the 8th century BCE in the Northern Kingdom of Israel, was concerned with social justice in what had become an urban society. A wealthy merchant class had emerged that secured its economic position at the expense of the poor (sound familiar?). The burden of prophetic complaint was a lack of moral leadership: the law courts served the interests of a commercial class and economic plenty for the few existed alongside poverty, inequality and injustice. These were the features that had produced moral atrophy. The monarchy centralised power and reorganised social relations, which damaged reciprocal obligation and weakened social and tribal ties contingent on the rise of a privileged class that prioritised the status symbols of economic advancement over an ethic of covenant responsibility for all. The result was a religious, social and moral decay that formed the burden of the prophetic message: social evil, the dishonesty and heartlessness of the rich, and indifference to the poor was an affront to Israel's history, tradition and culture that damaged the national character. In other words, the nation had departed from its covenant responsibilities towards each other.

Finally, at this juncture in these court proceedings, one of the most important philosophers of the Western philosophical tradition was summoned to give evidence to advance a deontological perspective to contest othering (Greek δεόν/*deon*, interpreted as duty, should or ought). Professor Kant's personal witness testimony was delivered to the court as follows.

Call Immanuel Kant into the witness box

> In order to advance the ethical proposition that duty and obligation towards the other person is a matter of intrinsic right, I argue that

moral concepts are *a priori* located in human reason. It is important to differentiate between what *is* the case, or the actualities of human behaviour, and what *ought* to be the case according to the logical progression of philosophical argument. The latter form of moral knowledge is *a priori* because it does not depend on observing or experiencing how people behave. Father Copleston (2003 [1960], pp 308–9) provided an explanation of the difference by suggesting that we cannot verify the statement that people ought to tell the truth by examining whether they do so or not. The statement is true independently of conduct that establishes an objective principle compelling to the human will, a command of reason that constitutes an *a priori* imperative. Let me ponder the concept of a good will, which has central importance when assembling the resources to contest the demonised and relegated other. A good will is good not because of what it produces or achieves, but by virtue of it being good in itself. In other words, it has intrinsic merit and value. It requires no qualification and nor can it be added to something else to produce bad results. Fundamentally, a good will, even if lacking in power to carry out its intentions, and even if it still accomplishes nothing by expending considerable effort, and only good will is left, would still shine like a jewel for its own sake as something that has full value in itself (Kant, 2005 [1785]). When politicians and organisational managers take an obsessive interest in achieving the 3Es of economy, efficiency and effectiveness, or exult in achieving value for money, I respond with my deontological ethic (duty) because I am primarily concerned with what is right rather than efficient and effective.

You will probably agree with me that the human condition is subjected to good and bad impulses, desires and drives, but a good will manifests itself in acting for the sake of duty in relation to others. Of course, there are many obstacles to exercising a good will and doing one's duty, but the moral law ought to be obeyed for its own sake. Further clarification is helpful at this point. It is possible to argue that access to higher truths is contained in the voice of duty. This inner voice is manifested in the claim of moral obligation towards others and has the force of a categorical imperative – the moral imperative to do what is right, not the imperative to enjoy. Of course, because my philosophy imposes limits on reason and knowledge, it is not possible to say with certainty that the inner voice, the demand of duty that is compelling to the will, comes from God. Do not forget that we are free to accept or reject this demand. Perhaps the best we can do is to suggest that morality, obligation and duty *intimate* the existence of a high truth, a transcendent order that we normally call God (Steiner, 1973, p 101).

Those human actions evaluated to contain moral worth must be performed out of reverence for the law. To repeat, moral worth is derived not from results, whether actual or intended, but from the motivation of the human agent. Nevertheless, this vocabulary of good will, duty and the moral law appear philosophically abstract and lacking in content. So, how do these abstract concepts translate into the concrete moral life? My answer introduces the aforementioned categorical imperative, which has three modes of expression:

- 'I ought never to act except in such a way that I can also will that my maxim should become a universal law' (Kant, 2005 [1785], p 15), for example, speak truth not lies;
- humanity is an end in itself – we cannot and must not use other human beings as the means by which we pursue and achieve our own ends. In other words, we must not relegate or demonise other people to accrue self-advantage; and
- what can be referred to as the universal legislative will.

Interestingly, the previous testimony of Dr Schweitzer argued that reverence for the moral law lacked existential human content when he stated that 'How far Kant is from understanding the problem of finding a basic moral principle which has a definite content can be seen from the fact that he never gets beyond an utterly narrow conception of the ethical' (Schweitzer, 1929, p 108). Consequently, he replaced my reverence for law with, as we heard earlier, reverence for life. Nevertheless, Dr Schweitzer's evaluation supported the centrality of human beings as ends rather than means, motives rather than consequences, so that all manifestations of manipulation and calculation (the utilitarian ethic) must abdicate before the demands of immediate and sovereign duty. My deontological ethical position, or ethic of duty, fundamentally rejects utilitarian ethics for a system demonstrable by abstract philosophical and theoretical arguments. It is more concerned with the ideal of pure reason than pragmatic and calculable decisions in complex human situations. Nevertheless, the central concepts of significance that I bring to the attention of this court, my primary vocabulary of interest, should not hastily be dismissed, which can be distilled as follows: *a priori*, good will, duty, motive, moral consciousness and obligation, moral law, ends over means, and respect for human personality. This is a vocabulary of terms assembled to contest pejorative othering.

The court adjourned again at this point to the reverberations of Kant and the possibility that God, a higher truth, masquerades as morality (Eagleton, 2009) in the demands of duty and claims of obligation. Of course, this is more a matter of faith than knowledge. Furthermore, the court adjourned to assimilate the personal witness testimonies of Schweitzer, Bonhoeffer, Küng, Anderson and Kant. This disparate evidence cogently contests the process and function of othering. The next stage in proceedings is for the court to reconvene in order to receive and digest a series of written documentary submissions exhumed from the historical record. This evidence, representative of different intellectual strands and traditions, can be presented through the following accounts.

Bundles of additional evidence submitted to the court

The Pauline letters on the new way of life

This body of work, comprised mainly of letters (epistolai) written in Greek from the 1st century CE by a Jew who claimed Roman citizenship, was influenced by, but also framed within, a Greek, Roman and Jewish framework of understanding. To understand this legacy, it is instructive to refer to the meticulous scholarship of Blumenfeld (2001), which situates Pauline theology within Platonic and Aristotelian politics. The significance of Blumenfeld's exegesis is in drawing attention to a neglected political dynamic in these letters. The Pauline letters stylistically resonate with Aristotle's *Ethics* in moving from the individual to the city, from ethics to politics. Like Aristotle, 'Paul connects one's proper end with the collective end, the good of one with that of the many, ethics with politics' (Blumenfeld, 2001, p 382; see also Taubes, 2004). The salient motif of this ethico-political perspective is the one body (*soma*) and its interconnected limbs, which unite the one and the many, self and other, into a collective unity of mutual coexistence. Furthermore, what is good is rooted in the concept of *dikaiosunē* (justice), a term that Plato used in the *Republic*. Specifically, *dikaiosunē* has a richer meaning than its English-translated usage because its subject matter is individual *and* social morality, which assimilates ethics and politics. Accordingly, *dikaiosunē* has a 'less legal and more moral meaning than justice. It is the Greek word for morality, personal quality, and right action' (Plato, 1974, p 65). It supports the Aristotelian virtues of wisdom, prudence and justice, but in the Pauline letters, *agapē* (love) is the essence of the new order of relations that defines citizenship. The conception of what is a fundamentally new political and ethical order transcends the construction of the *other* through eradicating socially constructed binaries. If (look again at Chapter One) the socio-symbolic order of the Roman Empire and many others before and since divided the state into us and them, patrician and plebeian, free and slave, men and women, and haves and have-nots, these binaries were transcended in Pauline thought in a radically new ethico-political dispensation where there would be neither Jew and Greek, Greek and barbarian, free and slave, wealthy and poor, or ruler and ruled. This was the good news. It is nothing less than an ethico-political and human transformation that is subversive, scandalous and revolutionary.

The symbolic representation of this transformed ethico-political existence is an unsettling cross (the Greek word is '*stauros*', mentioned earlier in the witness testimony). It should be noted that right at the beginning of Christianity is a sacrificial self-giving death that contests self-interest and the way in which the world is ordered and routinely functions. The sacrificial cross is the ultimate ethical expression of costly self-renunciation on behalf of the *other*. Consequently, Pauline ethics resonates with Hippodamos and Aristotle, who warned against the reproduction of social inequality on the platform of economic surfeit that benefits the few, and the changes to the social conditions of existence that they present to all of us (see Blumenfeld, 2001, p 388). It has been further explained that the scandalon of the New Testament presented in Paul's letters is that the new being that models existence on Bonhoeffer's man for others 'overturns all the social pride and convention of the surrounding culture' (Wright, 2009, p 26). It constitutes nothing less than a new narrative, producing a new person, wrapped within a new signification system. The wisdom of the world clashes with that of the new order of existence because 'the whole point of the gospel is to put the world – not upside down, because that is where it already is, but the right way up' (Wright, 2009, p 131). Everything is judged by different political and ethical criteria that demand a new perspective on all dimensions of life that reconcile politics, ethics and human subjectivity into a transcendent and universal unity. Indubitably, it directly contests the pejorative relegation and demonisation of the other and appeals for its elimination.

Homer's Iliad, Hector and living in the city

At this point, the jury is presented with a copy of Adam Nicholson's (2014) book *The mighty dead*, which offers a captivating assessment of Homer's *Iliad* (see ch 10, specifically 'The gang and the city'). This is pertinent to the theme of this monograph at this critical juncture in the evaluation of written evidence. It recounts the poignant death of Hector by Achilles and, in doing so, demarcates the geography of city and plain. The city of Troy is Hector and representative of goodness;

the plain is horror and terror, represented by the figure of Achilles (which resonates with the psychoanalytical orders of the Symbolic and Real alluded to earlier and to which we return shortly). The city, or polis, is the locale for Trojan families and community; the plain is Achilles, standing alone outside the city. Nicholson (2014, p 206) explains that the *Iliad* could have ended at the point where Hector is killed by Achilles and the attendant images of violence and death. This is not the last word because Troy is *agapē*, home, family, community and a shared humanity that tenuously clings to the face of the earth formed 4.5 billion years ago. This is suggestive of being immersed in the dramatics of life together and Troy is representative of, and the desire for, wholeness and Oneness, not the construction and reproduction of the excluded, denigrated and fractured demonised *other*.[1] To implement this Homeric vision of how all of us could belong to the earth, and live together in the city 12,000 years after the Agricultural Revolution and those early civilisations, demands an existential ethically informed political act to transform and transcend the current order of things. Specifically, it requires making the transition from self-interest to the public interest. En route, it is necessary to include Joyce and Eliot, which adds further fuel to an ethic of contestation.

From Troy to Dublin

James Joyce (see Kiberd, 2009) conveyed the moral vision in *Ulysses* (this modernist novel is structured by and mapped onto Homer's *Odyssey*) that public space in the polis, the mundane streets where people come into contact with each other during the course of daily routines, teach social relations between the self and others (Kiberd, 2009, p 246). The lesson in wisdom conveyed in the *Odyssey* that complements the *Iliad* is that nothing excels the ability of men and women to live together in harmony. If Homer heroicised Odysseus, Joyce domesticated Leopold Bloom to convey the heroic in the ordinary events and routine tasks of everyday life. In fact, 'The whole of Ulysses might be taken as just an extended hymn to the dignity of everyday living, when cast against the backdrop of a world war' (ie the First World War) (Kiberd, 2009, p 288). Consequently, the classics have the ability to inform reflection on a more humane order of existence, of how we are and could be attached to the earth and to each other. However, it depends on taking the decision to say 'Yes' to life, which is Schweitzer's affirmation of reverence for life, and 'Yes' to others, just as Bloom and Molly say 'Yes' to each other at the end of *Ulysses*. Additionally, according to the novelist George Eliot in *Middlemarch*, human relationships are unquestionably problematic but there is always the possibility to grow beyond the egoistic condition and imposed limitations of self-centredness. To paraphrase the Eliot of *Middlemarch*: 'If I really care for you – if I try to think myself into your position and orientation – then the world is bettered by my effort at understanding and comprehension' (Mead, 2014, p 223). Empathy and imaginative understanding attenuate egoism so that human growth is possible through openness to others, in taking the step from self to other, from the closed world of the ego to intersubjective relations. This requires a considerable effort to sustain. Decades before Eliot and Joyce, Adam Smith (1759), in *The theory of moral sentiments*, said that the expression of mutual sympathy was a virtue and human beings had the capacity to identify with the needs of others. It was too early to understand that the capitalist order would work against this virtue by elevating competition over cooperation.

Representatives of personalism laced with Kantian intimations

Personalist ethics is represented in the work of Berdyaev (1935), who endorsed a commitment to the intrinsic worth of human beings. This found support in Mounier (1952), where a Kantian morality of intrinsic ends takes priority over calculable means. Father Copleston (2003 [1975], p 310) reminds us that Mounier's ethics had its roots in the spiritualist tradition of French philosophy, which constituted a reaction to those 'intellectual and social-political tendencies which appear to treat man simply as an object of scientific study or to reduce him to his function in the economic sphere or in the social-political totality'. Additionally, Sartre's (1948) essay *Existentialism and humanism* suggested that the starting point for the philosophic enterprise is individual subjectivity. Put another way, this is the 'I', subjectivity and consciousness of Descartes (1596–1650). When we say 'I think' or 'I am', we are conscious of positioning the self in relation to the presence of the other, that is, from subjectivity to intersubjectivity. Accordingly, we can draw together the existentialist and humanistic insight of Sartre with the representatives of personalism, specifically the existence of the self in relation to the other. Personalism, for Mounier, has similarities to existentialism in its reaction to, for example, Hegel's philosophical system that relegates the individual to a fleeting moment in the history of what is referred to as the Absolute. In other words, Mounier rejects all systems of thought and practices that threaten humanity itself (as Schweitzer did earlier). Next, Buber's (1970) language of I–thou expresses holistic engagement between the self and other, in opposition to I–object–thing relations that create the conditions for othering. Buber writes of human existence as a personal encounter with others, dialogue and engagement between two separate beings, who meet under conditions of mutuality, reciprocity and equality. Finally, Levinas (see Hand, 1989, p 1) refers to the importance and significance of face-to-face relations as a fundamental ethical relation that transcends the tyranny of the ego. The personalist edifice radically contests the process and function of pejorative othering, the construction of the demonised and relegated other.

By connecting with Chapter Two, it may be observed that the constitution and functioning of organisations during the early years of the 21st century do not always conduce to face-to-face personal relations between I and you, self and other. The modern organisation can be an oppressive environment in which to work, involving the inescapable and relentless fusillade of emails, available 24 hours a day, that started to emerge around the year 2000. Arguably, they have a part to play in maintaining the efficient functioning of organisational routines, an efficient means by which to communicate information around the increasingly complex circuits of organisational life. However, they have contributed to the advancement of impersonal managerial bureaucracies that can damage personal relations (see discussion in Whitehead, 2016a). This is management via email correspondence rather than personal human contacts, a mixed blessing for organisational employees. Finally, Eagleton (2009, p 226) has acknowledged the harms inflicted by capitalist forces and relations, as well as postmodern culture, which have combined to erode socio-ethical human relations. This is anathema to the written submissions of Berdyaev, Mounier, Buber and Levinas. For these thinkers, 'Ethics is what hurts' (Eagleton, 2009, p 235) because of its stringent claims, demands and costs, which transcend all moves in the direction of relegating and demonising the other. Personalist ethics reconfigures relations between the self and other and contests the conditions of modern life, which are often *felt* as more impersonal than personal.

Lacan and Žižek and the three psychoanalytic orders of existence

The final chapter alludes to transcendental materialism, which draws upon the Lacanian–Žižekian psychic orders of the Imaginary, Symbolic and Real (see note 1 in Chapter One). Before doing so, it is helpful to take a more leisurely tour around psychoanalysis, radical politics and ethics to offer an account of these three orders.[2] The Lacanian *Imaginary* is complex, additionally complicated by competing assessments of the human condition (see Stevenson and Haberman, 1998). Lacan draws upon phenomenology, psychology and ethology to theorise the human psyche at the intersections of psychic disharmony, fragmentation and conflicting drives. The Imaginary is our lived experience of 'reality'. It appertains to identity and consciousness, our hopes, dreams and nightmares, and the mental images that we project to make sense of the chaotic bagatelle of invading psychic stimuli from the world in which we live. For Lacan, as well as Žižek, the Imaginary order presents a serious problem for the contemporary subjects of the postmodern era (Jameson, 1991), structured by global capitalism and consumer culture as the dominant signifiers of narcissistic self-obsession at the expense of the other (see Hall et al, 2008). Of course, this was acknowledged earlier: human beings are capable of demonstrating love of neighbour and doing their Kantian duty and exercising obligation towards others. Nevertheless, for Lacan and Žižek, the core of our being is a 'non-essential void of conflicting drives' (Hall and Winlow, 2015, p 109), rather than created by God and for God according to the doctrines of theology. How things turn out for us depends on early childhood influences, exposure to or avoidance of trauma, the pattern of socialisation, ideological assimilation, and the position we strike within a Symbolic order to enhance, or stifle, the best of human qualities that have implications for our relations with others.

The *Symbolic order* or *Big Other* is an invisible order that structures our experience of reality. It is the network of language, rules, regulations, rituals, myths and codes into which we are socialised or not. It is not 'given' with the world, or part of its essential fabric that emerged once the earth cooled down after the big bang 4.5 billion years ago, and it has no independent existence. Rather, it is symbolic in the sense that it is comprised of myths and scripts, but, at the same time, it is vital for our collective existence. Even though it does not 'exist' and is not 'real', we must believe in it as though it were real (like God), invest faith in it to give life meaning and value as we proceed from a state of Hobbesian raw nature to culture and ethics. It is the gloss, or facade, we require in order to fashion the contours of civilisation that make it possible for human beings to coexist alongside each other. Importantly, if the fragmented and alienated Lacanian subject is the product of an arbitrary signification-language system, then the Symbolic order is not a permanently fixed structure, but open to transformative manipulation (Myers, 2003, p 24). Change the system structure, its material and ideological components, and you transform the conditions of existence for the subject. It is possible for the subject to exist within, to reflect and to reproduce different Symbolic orders of existence, which is pertinent when exploring pejorative othering. Consistent with the recurring theme of this monograph, the central ethico-cultural task is to proceed from the rituals of pejorative othering towards building a Symbolic order, or Big Other, that reduces othering.

The Lacanian *Real* is not synonymous with 'reality'. If reality consists of symbols – the constituent elements of a signification system arbitrarily imposed on the world rather than essentially given

– then the 'Real is the unknown that exists at the limits of this socio-symbolic universe and is in constant tension with it' (Homer, 2005, p 81). If the Imaginary is alienation, deception, fragmentation and the order of narcissistic identification, and the Symbolic is the order of language, law and culture that fashions the human subject, then the Real is located outside the Symbolic. In other words, the Real is the experiential enigmatic and traumatic at the heart of the subject and, according to Eagleton (2009, p 141), the 'gash in our being where we were torn loose from the maternal body, and from which desire flows unstaunchably'. It is both vacuous and 'horrifically enjoyable' (Eagleton, 2009, p 143). The Real is shock, awe, trauma, a gaping wound, violence and the gash that 'destabilises our entire universe of meaning. As such, the Real can only be discerned in its traces, effects and after shocks' (Žižek, 2014, pp 119–20). In psychoanalytic language, it is the Real that relegates and demonises the other.

When transposing these three Lacanian psychoanalytical categories into a political register, Žižek utilises Hegel's dialectical methodology, Marx's critique of capitalism and Lacanian psychoanalysis (Myers, 2003). Elliot (2005, p 184) comments that 'Žižek's writing, stranded somewhere between high modernism and postmodern pastiche, can be viewed as an attempt to develop a psychosocial diagnosis of the self in its dealings with the global capitalist economy'. For Žižek, the postmodern world has fashioned a subject riddled with doubt, anxiety and insecurity, uncoupled from fixed universal anchoring points in the transition from the post-war Keynesian settlement to the neoliberal politico-economic order. Additionally, postmodernity signals the decline of the Symbolic order as the framework of collective meanings, intersubjectivity and mutuality, essential if human beings are not to be reduced to self-indulgence at the expense of the other. The postmodern subject is involved in narcissistic identification and ego obsessions, pursues stupid pleasures at the expense of substantive meanings and values, and, in doing so, reflects and reproduces the capitalist-neoliberal order. The response, inspired by Marxist critique, requires an ethical and political transformative act to establish a Symbolic order of civilised interpersonal relations based on cooperation rather than conflict. To state the matter differently, it is the critical shift from raw nature to human culture that constitutes the Symbolic order that enables social life in all its meaningful communication and committed human relationships (Winlow and Hall, 2013). We must continue to make the leap from self to other, ego to social, state of nature to state of culture, to become a person alongside other persons. Eagleton (2009, p 6) clarifies that Lacan derived his thought from Hegel, for whom 'the transition from one state to another has an ethical dimension'. Žižek, elevated to the high priesthood of atheistic theology, states: 'I think this is the legacy of Christianity – this legacy of God not as a big Other or guarantee but God as the ultimate ethical agency who puts the burden on us to organise ourselves' (Žižek, 2010, p 180). This is Badiou's universalism and Schweitzer's and Bonhoeffer's ethic of responsibility for others, which stands in marked opposition to all forms of anti-ethical arrangements that produce the relegated and demonised *other*. To pick up on something we looked at earlier, it is immoral to avoid responsibility for others. If we are serious about dealing head-on with the problematic of othering as a contingent and harmful occurrence, rather than something immutably given with human existence, we need to progress in the final evidential submission from immorality to the moral, through the concept of moral economy that refines some earlier work (Whitehead, 2015a).

Moral economy: a device to analyse, critique, contest and replace othering

Personal witness statements addressed to the slaughter bench of history that we considered earlier, supplemented by a collection of written submissions, combine to assemble some of the multilayered resources to excavate the concept of the moral to contest *othering*. There is much for the jury to consider in its deliberations. The next step integrates statements and diverse bundles of evidence into the conceptual device of moral economy. Moral economy has affinities with the Weberian *ideal type*, a methodological procedure to compensate for investigative limitations in the social sciences. If social phenomena are ambiguous and cannot be observed directly, as Durkheim suggested, the ideal type is constructed to identify the relevant properties of what is subjected to investigation. Accordingly, moral economy, as conceptual device or ideal type, accentuates certain features of reality. It is a caricature related to reality but not its exact representation. It functions as an interpretive device, is an elucidatory procedure, identifies traits, advances comparative analysis and can be put to work to expose intellectual and moral deficiency in the construction of the *other*, with all its serious implications for political economy, personal relations, organisational life and national and international relations.

There is little doubt that the concept of moral economy is complex, can be contested and is ambiguous. Nevertheless, it is a concept that repays careful consideration (on its conceptual history, see Götz, 2015). Moral economy asserts the unconditional value of human life on planet earth. We have just recounted how Schweitzer's anthropocentric ethic advanced a life view, where the primary principle of the moral is reverence for life, a position supported by other testimonies recounted in this chapter. This is the platform upon which to conduct human relations, its sphere of interest encapsulating just and right dealings with each other. It is a life view with micro (individual subjectivity), mezzo (institutional) and macro (political-economy) dimensions. The content of moral economy is enriched by: Kant's ethic of duty (or deontological ethic, see Whitehead, 2016b), which prioritises human beings in a kingdom of ends, not calculable means; Weberian substantive rationality, not instrumental rationality, as the motivation for social action; and benevolence as valued more highly than egoistic self-interest. This requires a decisive, undoubtedly difficult, yet necessary move from the self to the other to establish intersubjective social relations of mutuality, empathy and trust. When Schweitzer issued the invitation in the aftermath of the catastrophic First World War to 'look for a human being or some work devoted to human welfare' (Schweitzer, 1929, p 260), Bonhoeffer's ethical injunction required human beings to emulate the man for others. All of us are confronted with obligations towards others during the routine practices of daily life, practising reverence for life and endorsing a personalist outlook that disturbingly contests the production of the relegated and demonised other. As mentioned earlier, individuals and families undoubtedly engage in the tenets of moral economy despite living under conditions of neoliberal capitalism, which is indifferent to morality. However, if we want to reduce othering consistent with the central theme of this monograph, political economy must be transformed by moral economy, in other words, a Symbolic order or socio-symbolic system of a completely different order to the neoliberal capitalist era.

Schweitzer and Bonhoeffer on the nature of human existence and philosophical ethics, Küngian theology and Christology, Pauline epistolary resources appertaining to political ethics, the Judaeo-Christian Old and New Testament inheritance, and entreaties on personalism, existentialism and the Symbolic order with Lacan and Žižek, all these resources inform moral economy and draw attention towards the ethico-cultural significance of being men and women for others as the definitive norm of responsibility and maturity that radically resists all attempts at relegating and demonising others. It is committed to *agapē* (love), which is a scandal because it represents a radical challenge to the organisation of life immersed in self-interest, extracting from others to benefit the self. Love contests lives rooted in self-interest. The point is that all citizens matter and socially constructed binary distinctions, the differential allocation of material resources that reproduce inequality, and the signs and symbols of material success and status must be transcended by a decisive ethico-political act to transform the conditions of existence. Transcendence is achieved through commitment to a higher unity that, for some, is the theologian's God or Other, and for others, is a Symbolic order, or Big Other, that fashions a human subjectivity different to that required by the capitalist system through attachment to an alternative set of values. Moral economy makes demands, requires existential choices and is sacrificially costly in how we utilise human resources and spend our time. It functions within the circuits of a value system where it is preferable to give than receive, where relations are based on *agapē*, not exchange, and where humanity is one and not divided by the cult of narcissistic hyper-individualism and its consumerist socio-symbolic system that snags all of us in its web. It is in marked contrast to a political, economic and social organisation that advances an elite at the expense of others in order to maintain a competitive advantage at the expense of others.

To repeat, its operating symbol is a sacrificial and renunciatory cross, not the status symbols of material excess and its shimmering objects so highly prized by consumer culture and its media outlets. It is dialogic, face-to-face engagement between self and others, and it is as absurd and scandalous as unorthodox. It cuts against the grain by challenging *the way the world is* in arguing for justice (*dikaiosunē*), fairness, equality and the virtues of moral excellence and goodness. Moral economy is committed to further the good life in the city with Hector rather than Achilles. Moral economy is *agapē*, service and the capacity for self-sacrifice. Although human beings act from questionable motives, we are nevertheless capable of sympathy, benevolence and, as Adam Smith (2009 [1759]), among others, deduced, showing an interest in the fortune of others. We are not born with these qualities, but we do have the potential to exercise them if nurtured properly by responsible others under the right conditions of existence. Not to do this is a persistent threat to the stability of the socio-moral order and our ability to coexist alongside each other.

Concluding comments on ethical contestation

The resources presented in this chapter, distilled from a cloud of witnesses, stimulate thinking on duty to and moral obligation for the demonised and relegated other. They have implications for the conditions of existence under which we currently live and contest the modernised and transformed criminal justice system (Whitehead, 2016a). These resources can be assimilated into the concept of moral economy that contests the neoliberal reconstruction of criminal justice, as exemplified in the privatisation of probation on the platform of competition and marketisation. If the 'writings of Marx, Weber and Durkheim, in their varying ways, fuse together an analysis and a moral critique of modern society' (Giddens, 1971, p 224), the concept of moral economy fuses together analysis and critique of the moral collapse of the criminal justice system exemplified in the modernisation, transformation and privatisation of probation services. This is the context for the excavation of the relegated and demonised other. It needs to be restated, as this point is in danger of being forgotten, that probation services should not solely be evaluated or valued for what they achieve – the instrumental goal of reducing reoffending. They should also be valued for what they stand for, which is an ethical ideal when working with people who offend, most of whom have a complicated biological, psychological and sociological life story to recount. Within the context of discussing moral theories of the 18th-century Enlightenment – Shaftesbury, Hutcheson, Butler, Smith, Hume and Kant – Copleston (2003 [1958], p 39) said that a 'materialist interpretation of man' did not reject moral ideals and principles. Diderot, for example, drew attention to the ideal of self-sacrifice and demanded benevolence, pity and altruism from human beings. Equally, D'Holbach made morality a matter of altruism in the service of the common good. We must listen to these voices from our intellectual heritage.

Eagleton's (2009) contribution to ethical enquiry includes a number of references to the other, as well as Hegel. Autonomy and freedom can only flourish in the context of social life and engagement with others through reciprocity and mutual cooperation, which is opposed to lives of Nietzschean solitude. Accordingly, both 'Hegel and Marx acknowledge that the subject and its end are constituted by its relations with others' (Eagleton, 2009, p 125) but under specific conditions of existence. Consequently, it is Hegel who 'recognises that morality must be a question of social organisation, not simply isolated individual wills' (Eagleton, 2009, p 126). The fulfilment of each person is fundamentally the condition for the fulfilment and well-being of all. For Eagleton (2009, p 126), it is extremely hard 'to think of a more precious form of ethics'. It is said that Alexander the Great 'dreamed of "one world" – a world bound together by Greek culture' (Anderson, 1988, p 612). By contrast, the One humanity articulated in the Pauline letters turned everything upside down, including Alexander's Macedon and the Roman Empire, because its ethico-cultural foundation was *agapē* and not power, violence and conflict, as illustrated in Chapter One. The prerequisite of the new order of existence endorsed the other as neighbour, not enemy to be conquered and vanquished. For us, the moment is now and must be seized to confront and contest othering in all its forms, including the critical questioning of the demonised and relegated other of criminal justice organisation. Of course, we are up against it, we feel the crushing weight of the stream of history in full spate, but whose side are we on? Are we going to give the last word to the slaughter bench of history that continues to stoke the charnel house boiler? Or, are we going to choose a different future? In other words, are we going to resist or collaborate with the reproduction of othering and its associated conditions of existence? Resistance or collaboration remains the ethical question that all of us must answer.

Leaders and prime ministers consistently make their predictable evangelical pitch to exhort a politics of good news, particularly at the point of election and coronation, to create a country that *works for the benefit of all* and where no one will be left behind. The attraction of a break with the past, the beginning of a new beginning, is repeatedly dangled before us. Undoubtedly, this is a noble aspiration, but it is all too often wrapped in the wrinkled skin of vacuous rhetoric. The natural logic of the neoliberal capitalist order of things that shows no sign of dissipating is that it does not work, it cannot work, equally for all. The profit motive and exchange relation will ensure that. Therefore, the current system will be maintained, there will be more of the same and we will all end up disappointed once again. There will be no ethically driven political transformation that is required to create a country that *works for the benefit of all*. However, the point is that there could be if this is what we are minded to achieve. The critical question is how to transcend othering, to move beyond our analysis and critique of how this occurs in order to establish new conditions of existence to reduce, if not eliminate, the production and reproduction of the pejorative other, as ethically contested in this chapter. I must admit that the omens are not at all favourable when we are force-fed a diet of 'take back control', 'Make America great again', 'Austria first' during the presidential election of December 2016 and the troubling realities of Europe (Murray, 2017) – agendas dominated more by economic imperatives than ethical priorities. This is the issue for discussion and resolution in the final chapter, to which we should now turn.

Notes

[1] This is a reference to Greek philosophy that contextualises Homer. In other words, there was a problem of the One and the Many in pre-Socratic philosophy that required a resolution. Later, in post-Aristotelian philosophy (see Copleston, 2003 [1946], p 488), Stoicism emphasised the One, a cosmic pantheism, and Epicureanism the Many, which appeared in a 'cosmology built on an atomistic basis and in a (theoretically at least) egoistic ethic'.

[2] Lacan's (2001) *Écrits* is a useful place to look, particularly: seminar II (1978) and the early formulation of the Symbolic order and how the subject is constituted by and within a chain of signification; seminar VII (1986), which is important for the social sciences and humanities; and seminar XI (1973), which is indubitably complex (see also Homer, 2005) . For a lucid explanation of the three orders, see Winlow and Hall (2013) *Rethinking social exclusion*, particularly the glossary. It is also instructive to look at Žižek (1992, 2006, 2014).

FOUR

Transcending the other: moral economy and universal ethics

As we edge towards a resolution of the demonised other excavated in this monograph from a wider historical to a narrower criminal justice perspective, let us advance some further apposite reflections. Plato divided 'reality' into our world of everyday experience and a transcendent other world. He pondered a separate dimension of reality set apart from our transient daily lives. This separation introduced into the Western intellectual tradition the idea that our world is an imperfect copy of the transcendent realm, with the attendant danger of denigration. Plato influenced the Judaeo-Christian tradition of our world and another beyond the bright blue sky, earth and heaven, imminent and transcendent, Being and becoming. This was a world view that also contained the potential to denigrate the world in which we live. The better, more perfect and ideal were pushed in the direction of a separate order of reality, not the here and now. Next, the history of the crusades from 1095 to 1291 (Asbridge, 2010) exposed and exacerbated religious and political fault lines between Christian West and Muslim East.[1] These crusading adventures demonised the religious other, which continues into the 21st century with such devastating consequences. The willingness to harm those who belong to different religious, cultural and ethnic traditions is as persistent as it remains obscene. It is a bloody stream of history that chokes with infamy and that we are unable to resolve. Furthermore, 200 years after the end of the fourth crusade, the Reformation and Counter-Reformation released psychotic energies of religious extremism into 'Christian Europe', where Catholic and Protestant tried to destroy each other in the name of the 'true' faith that each side of the religious divide claimed to possess. The violent destruction of the religious other was a perversion of the aforementioned Pauline vision of One humanity. As far as I know, there are no Protestants or Catholics in the New Testament canon, only an invitation to be part of One, universal humanity on earth. Finally, Kant split reality into phenomena and noumena before Hegel's correction affirmed that reality is one and not splintered into a thousand philosophical, religious and political pieces.

If we splice the illustrations from the historical record in Chapter One with criminal justice in Chapter Two, to the additional references just cited, it is easy to conclude that Homo sapiens have excelled at constructing dislocated fault lines. Our ancestors have bestowed a complex legacy that reaches into the present. However, what has been constructed in thought (ideology) and by deed (behaviour) can be dismantled. Undoubtedly, it is a tall order to step into the stream of history to divert its course. Nevertheless, it should be our urgent task to re-conjugate this less than edifying historical record, supported by the ethical resources assimilated in the previous chapter. Just because it is like it is does not mean that it has to persist in its present form. The current orthodoxy is a contingent creation, not a permanently fixed condition. There is always an alternative. Sinking ethical shafts of confrontation into the current order of things remains an existential possibility to shake the foundations of pejorative othering, to reset our present course. Plainly, our collective future does not have to reproduce the past.

From framing the other in Chapter One, to engaging with the demonised and relegated other of the modernised criminal justice system under specific politico-economic conditions in Chapter Two, to considering diverse ethico-cultural resources that contest pejorative othering in Chapter Three, we are invited to reconsider our duties and obligations towards each other. Support for this ethical injunction is evidenced in the previous chapter by summoning a rich body of resources to appear before the slaughter bench of history. The ethical invitation to exercise obligation towards others must be taken seriously if we want to coexist according to the basic tenets of reverence for life. Capitalist longevity, sustained by its latest mutation in neoliberalism, with its deadly global embrace, has carved affective changes into human subjectivity that affect personal relations, family life, organisations and international relations. Personal relationships, family and community life depend upon a supporting platform of nourishing values: mutual obligation, give and take, trust, commitment, even a sacrificial act of self-renunciation to benefit others. These are the components of a moral economy more than political economy. Moral economy is the stone in the shoe of neoliberal political economy that exalts the profit motive, taking out more than it puts in. Loving and nurturing personal–family–community relations at their best accommodate difference. They do not engage in the pejorative process and function of reproducing the demonised and relegated other. However, the neoliberal operating system is invasive, creating opportunities for pejorative othering (see Whitehead and Hall, forthcoming). This is evidenced in the transient shift from post-war Keynesian social democracy to the neoliberal order, as well as in criminal justice, where we have witnessed the erosion of probation services by the ideology of competition, privatisation, marketisation and a soulless bureaucracy (Whitehead, 2016a). We are left coping with a barren wastescape of economy, efficiency, effectiveness, value for money and a monochrome culture that manages more than it understands the lives of others. Schweitzer, Bonhoeffer, Judaeo-Christian ethics, personalism, existentialism, Bauman and the aforementioned ethically inspired representatives join forces to argue that it is immoral to avoid a duty for and obligation towards other human beings. The challenge is thrown down to be men and women for others because the neighbour is in close proximity; it could be anyone who needs me here and now. These obligations are more difficult to discharge under current political and economic operating conditions. There are considerable tensions, constant dilemmas and the clashing cymbals of confrontation between politico-economic and ethico-cultural ways of life. We remain confronted with prejudice and bigotry, religious and ethnic conflicts, and multiple harms inflicted on others depicted as enemies rather than neighbours (on race-hate incidents following the European Union referendum of 23 June 2016, see Shipman, 2016, p 457). Žižek, when talking about refugees earlier, powerfully argues for an immediate European response; the choice is between civilised actions or barbarism (but see the thesis of Murray, 2017).

In addition to the immediate claim of duty towards the other as our neighbour, it is equally important to move beyond the present to establish alternative conditions of existence. This involves immersion in an alternative ideology to the neoliberal order. This cannot happen overnight – it is a long process not a one-off event – but we must begin this transition at some point if we want to enhance our chances of living together. It is urgent and vital that we give ourselves a chance. To pursue this longer-term goal, it is necessary to embark on a detour into *transcendental materialism*, oxygenated by the previously considered three orders of the Imaginary, Symbolic and Real. This excursion demonstrates the possibility of changing the conditions of existence to reduce relegating others. If the process and function of othering has multiple causes – biological deficiencies, faulty socialisation, religious fault lines, ethnic conflicts, the weight of history and how we organise ourselves politically and economically – these must be transformed to reduce pejorative othering. Hearts and minds have to be redirected and relocated. According to transcendental materialism, it is possible to transform the presenting conditions of existence to offer hope to the genus Homo sapiens. Are we sufficiently interested to think about this to entertain the possibility of a future better than the past?

From transcendental idealism to transcendental materialism

Transcendental materialism is a psychosocial framework that draws on the three orders of Imaginary, Symbolic and Real alluded to earlier.

It suggests the possibility of transforming the political, economic and social conditions that structure human experience. If our desires and drives are contingent upon the social structure to which we belong, it is possible to change it and us. For example, capitalism is a socio-symbolic system characterised by egoistic individualism, fearful competition and advancing the self at the expense of the other. However, it is conceivable to establish a different socio-symbolic system that prioritises cooperation, solidarity and universality, where the other person is our neighbour and not disposable enemy. This means coming to a new agreement on *symbolic efficiency*, that is, a new agreement about what is of value in human life in order to create the civilised conditions of existence.

Let us track back to Bertrand Russell (1946, p 639), who described Immanuel Kant as the founder of German idealism, which asserts that reality is conceived in mental terms. Idealism prioritises the role of the mind and ideas. Solomon (1988) refers to Kant's 'transcendental pretence', the assumption of universality and necessity in our experience of human life. In other words, the transcendental self or ego 'determines the structure of our everyday experience' (Solomon, 1988, p 29), which implies that all human beings are gripped by fixed and unalterable categories of understanding.[2] By contrast, transcendental materialism asserts that our brains are not 'fixed' in the Kantian fashion, but instead hard-wired for plasticity and malleability. It is possible for human beings to adapt to different environments or Symbolic orders. If human subjects have been immersed into, and adapted to, the capitalist order of things over many centuries (Hall, 2014), this can be reversed by a process of 'deaptation'. Different Symbolic orders, or socio-symbolic systems, require and fashion different human subjectivities. Transcendental materialism draws attention to the interface between our experience as human beings, our prevailing culture and ideology, and our material-biological-neurological system. The thesis is neatly put like this:

> If genetics are weak in the areas of the complex emotional desires that connect drives with symbolism and external reality

in a two-way formative process, experience and ideology can be engraved in neuronal networks. With our flexible neurology, human beings are geared for deaptation and malleability. (Hall, 2012, p 253)

The human subject, starting life as a non-essential void or blank slate, is capable of good and evil. However, how we turn out depends on the conditions of existence established by the prevailing Symbolic order. The result, as Hall explains, would be to engrave different modes of experience and ideology into neuronal circuits and networks. Unless and until we engage in this transformative process, fertile conditions of existence for pejorative othering will persist. I want to illustrate this thesis by turning, first, to the Big Society and, second, to the language of reform applied to the criminal justice system. I want to argue that it is not possible to establish a Big Society or reform the criminal justice system unless and until fundamental ethical and political transformations occur at the level of the socio-symbolic system. We either carry on as we are and pretend current orthodoxy is both inevitable and normal, or change for the good of all.

A Big Society – 'you'll be lucky'

After May 2010, Coalition government politics aimed to make it 'easier for people to come together to improve their communities and help one another' (HM Government, 2010a, p 29; see also HM Government, 2010b), an aspiration endorsed at the very core of government because of its visionary simplicity that was thought to be catching on (Cabinet Office, 2010a). It advocated localism, enhancing communities through voluntary action, the development of a national citizen service, supporting cooperatives, mutuals and charities, and a Big Society bank to fund social investment projects from the proceeds of dormant accounts. At first view, its appeal was plausible and should not pose insurmountable difficulties when considering the merits of a concept that had acquired thematic relevance in England. Therefore, a prima facie case exists that the Big Society is replete with good intentions to bolster the social, which is 'another name for agreeing and sharing' (Bauman, 2001, p 2). It seemed to be the antidote to pejorative othering.

The Big Society was cited in *A stronger society: Voluntary action for the 21st century* (Conservative Party, 2008; for an assessment of its historical lineage, see Civil Exchange, 2013; see also New Economics Foundation, 2010). Subsequently, the Conservative Party (2010, p 37) manifesto elucidated that it signified the diminution of central government through enhancing local voluntarism, charitable giving and philanthropic action. These disparate elements were soldered together into Coalition government policy after the 2010 general election by blending the subject of conservative politics, who is free to select the path of sociocultural responsibility, with liberal-democratic civil liberties (HM Government, 2010a). A contingent feature of the Big Society was to redirect state-financed public services towards marketised competition from the private sector, including opportunities for the voluntary sector, by relocating organisations from what remains of the Keynesian state complex onto a different material platform (HM Government, 2010b; on 'payment by results', see Whitehead, 2015b). Precipitated by the latest bout of global economic turbulence that erupted in 2007–08, which legitimated an austerity package to resolve the crisis by reducing public expenditure (Stuckler and Basu, 2013, p 132), innovative action was considered necessary to respond to fiscal travails by the counterbalance of a compensatory appeal towards the social and ethical. Accordingly, the 'age of austerity' enabled Coalition politics to take advantage of the crisis to reconfigure the operations of late capitalism (see Mirowski, 2013), so that the 'contraction of the state through "fiscal discipline" is only part of a wider project affecting every part of society' (Douzinas, 2013, p 11), which frames the appeal to the Big Society. Far from being a simple idea designed to enhance the social, the concept can be constructed as a primary signifier of the state's strategic withdrawal from the social-public domain in order to build an alternative welfare system within civil society (Rodger, 2013, p 726). It is also grammatically abstruse because the Big Society is not an indicative or imperative verb form conjugated into clear lines of activity to be undertaken by me, you, us or them. Nevertheless, in the language of helping one another that embodies a legitimate appeal to the reorientation of the self's cognitive and emotional capacity for beneficence towards the other, the Big Society resonates with an aspirational social dynamic in marked contrast to egoistic individualism.

Even though, by the autumn of 2013, the politics of welfare benefits, immigration from Eastern Europe and education and criminal justice reform were diverting attention away from the Big Society, its appeal continued to attract both critical and positive comment (Civil Exchange, 2013; see also Cameron, 2013). A summation of pertinent references commences with the aforementioned *A stronger society* (Conservative Party, 2008). Since 2010, numerous governmental documents have purported to elucidate its conceptual appeal (Conservative Party, 2010; HM Government, 2010a, 2010b), supported by the Cabinet Office (2010a, 2010b). Notwithstanding these political supports, Maskell (2010), a UNITE union national officer, questioned the composition of the volunteer and mentor cohort, as well as the financial resources that would be required to facilitate the Big Society in an age of austerity. The National Council for Voluntary Organisations (2010) issued a briefing on the subject, the New Economics Foundation (2010) explored its historical lineage and the then prime minister articulated its political saliency in the Liverpool speech of 19 July 2010 (Cabinet Office, 2010a). Furthermore, what for Hilton, a former director of strategy at Downing Street, illustrates weaning the country off welfare dependency is more critically 'not about shared responsibility or equal partnership, or mutual exchange, but replacement, even obliteration', of the remaining vestige of the post-war Keynesian social protection state (New Economics Foundation, 2010, p 11). Boulton and Jones (2010, p 26) suggested that the Big Society did not take off as expected because rather than articulating a clear vision, it remained conceptually oblique. These authors included a reference to Peter Mandelson's assessment that 'had it been properly stress tested [it] would have been found to be unexplainable and unpersuasive' (Boulton and Jones, 2010, p 27), which echoes the theological analysis that it is 'aspirational waffle' (Williams, 2012). Stuckler and Basu (2013, p 132) take up the theme of austerity by clarifying that the chancellor of the Coalition government announced a fiscal reduction package of £83 billion, which would extract resources from nearly all government departments. Austerity shrank the role and responsibility of the state by reducing public spending, which, in turn, initiated radical reforms to what were once understood as the personal social services (Sainsbury, 1977). Consequently, the Big Society was conceived as taking up the slack by activating local community volunteers who will be animated into performing socially beneficent behaviour.

Jordan (2010), Rhodes (2011) and Ishkanian and Szreter (2012), on the *Big Society debate*, are also instructive texts. Specifically, Norman (2010) scans the disparate themes of politics, economics, philosophy, history, business, civil liberties, education and culture that are assembled to form the intellectual parameters within which to advance a defence of the Big Society. Norman, a conservative politician, offers a contemporary reworking of political liberalism and the supporting pillars of empowerment, freedom and individual responsibility to justify its appeal. What was a *simple* idea for Prime Minister Cameron is an *exciting* idea for Norman, but neither engaged critically to expose conceptual difficulties or policy inconsistencies. Finally, the Third Sector Research Centre (Lindsey and Bulloch, 2013) produced empirical research findings from 100 'observers', of whom 71 expressed a view on the Big Society: eight were ambivalent and eight were positive, but there were 55 negative responses. It is recorded that 'The primary ground on which the Big Society is criticized is that it is a political stunt' (Lindsey and Bulloch, 2013, p 8) to win elections and to function as a mask for public spending cuts. Accordingly, 'A key finding of this analysis is that the majority of observers who voiced an opinion on the matter held negative attitudes towards the Big Society agenda' (Lindsey and Bulloch, 2013, p 17). In summary, a number of positions adopted in response to the Big Society theme within the literature positively endorse localism, community empowerment and the benefits of individual responsibility. By contrast, others perceive a politically constructed veneer applied over reductions in public expenditure contingent upon the state's withdrawal from its civic responsibilities (Gosling, 2012; Civil Exchange, 2013; Rodger, 2013). What is more, even though Liverpool was in the vanguard of pilot areas for the Big Society in England (the others were Eden, Cumbria, Sutton, Greater London, Windsor and Maidenhead), it withdrew in February 2011 for lack of adequate funds. This brief survey of the literature confirms that it does not adequately address the Big Society located within political and economic developments and associated ethical implications that have relentlessly advanced since the neoliberal turn during the 1980s. Nor does the literature confront sufficiently the consequences of capitalist reconstruction and market expansion on organisations after 2010, which is a serious intellectual omission.

The Big Society enjoins people to help one another through reconfiguring our cognitive and emotional relations with each other. The appeal to build a Big Society is as laudable as it is aspirational. It resonates with the objective of *building a society that works for all*, the language of Prime Minister May during the election campaign of May/June 2017. However, it is not feasible to build a Big Society on neoliberal foundations that support a market society (Sandel, 2012) because they represent two irreconcilable socio-symbolic orders, ideological supports and substantive values. Neoliberal capitalism fashions and requires a form of human subjectivity and organisations that are in conflict with the requirements of a Big Society. Prevailing conditions of existence militate against a Big Society, just as they militate against the well-being of all. These conditions of existence can, of course, be *regulated* (post-war Keynesian dispensation), and regulation is better than no regulation or the 'big bang' deregulation of the 1980s. However, the operating conditions of capitalism cannot be *reformed*. It is not possible to graft a Big Society onto a capitalist platform. It is not possible to produce classic claret to rival Bordeaux in the North of England because the terroir does not exist. In order to move forward, a *transformative* ethico-political act is required that has fundamental implications for political economy, organisations and human subjectivity. Transcendental materialism and the aforementioned discussion on the three orders of the Imaginary,

Symbolic and Real provide a way forward beyond the current state of affairs by suggesting the possibility of change. Where does this leave our thinking on criminal justice and penal policy after the discussion in Chapter Two?

Criminal justice: the attraction and delusion of reformism

Applied to criminal justice, the language of reform is problematic and requires careful excavation, which can be illustrated as follows. Between 16 and 18 March 2016, I attended the Howard League for Penal Reform International Conference on 'Justice and reform: reshaping the penal landscape'. The event was held at Keble College, Oxford University, to which I contributed the paper 'From reformism to transformation: reflections on morality and justice'. Although attracted to the aspirational sentiment of reform, just as much as the Big Society, it presents problems. The alternative position that I advocated was informed by 30 years of working within the criminal justice system that began in 1977 as a probation volunteer. I subsequently worked as a probation officer in North-East England from 1981 to 2007, since when I have assimilated the experiences of practice to inform academic work at Teesside University from 2007 to 2018.

My thesis is that the criminal justice system cannot be reformed, and nor can the neoliberal platform that supports it. Rather, system and platform must be *transformed* by a foundational ethico-political act. How is it feasible to reform criminal justice when it has been subjected to repeated acts of destabilisation by the forces of neoliberal capitalism that the system increasingly reflects and reproduces? If we can learn anything from recent historical events, it is that we urgently need a different starting point, to alter our thinking, approach and response, and to shift the debate from reformism to substantive transformation. In other words, we need to transcend rather than collude with the current orthodoxy that has expanded since the 1980s and put us all on the back foot. Reformism is undoubtedly attractive because it suggests constructive activity, and, at times, I have associated myself with it. It adopts the position that doing something is better than doing nothing.

However, *something* rather than nothing often amounts to tinkering at the edges, piecemeal adjustments, a twist here, a nudge there and responding to the consequences of others' decisions when what is required is the foundational transformation of the politico-economic system that has rerouted criminal justice in a discernibly troubling direction during the previous 30 years – punishment, prison expansion, competition, private interests and the imposition of an internal market involving public, private and voluntary organisations.

The Conference was organised as a response to extensive and intrusive governmental decisions that have accumulated since the 1980s: the 1992–93 Prison Works volte-face; the 1997–2010 era of New Labour modernisation; and the 2010–15 rehabilitation revolution. The Conference was, self-evidently, talking not about more of the same, but something very different. It wanted to respond to, take issue with and reform attitudes towards retributive punishment, expanding prisons, community sentences and probation privatisation. However, the reforming impulse is as honourable as misguided unless it confronts the politico-economic, ideological and material forces of the generative and reproductive core of neoliberal capitalism that is indifferent to ethics and reform. This is the tune that we have been forced to dance to in the criminal justice domain for far too long (as well as other organisations) that limits the scope for reformism.

John Ruskin (1819–1900), mentioned earlier, was a student at Oxford and the first Slade Professor of Fine Art in 1869. There is a Ruskin College in Oxford. He was associated with the Pre-Raphaelites – Hunt, Millais and Rossetti – and Hunt's *Light of the world* can be found in Keble College chapel. In 1853, the acme of Victorian liberalism, Ruskin wrote that the 'whole system of modern society, politics, and religion seems to me so exquisitely absurd that I know not where to begin about it, or to end' (Batchelor, 2000, p 234). After 40 years working within, reflecting on and writing about criminal justice matters, in addition to attending conferences addressing the subject of reformism, Ruskin's comment can be applied to the state of criminal justice. Let us recount, albeit briefly, a recent history of the *exquisitely absurd*:

- It has been reconstituted by a mix of contradictory penal and political impulses. For example, it endorses an empirically supported policy of 'What Works', yet tolerates relatively high reconviction rates. Specifically, 46% of adults are reconvicted within one year of release from prison and over two thirds (68%) of those under 18 are reconvicted within a year of release (Prison Reform Trust, 2016). 'What Works' does not always do so.
- Between June 1993 and June 2012, the prison population in England and Wales increased by 41,800 to over 86,000. The projected prison population is 90,000 by 2020. Moreover, imprisonment rates in the UK are the highest in Western Europe, at 147 per 100,000 of the population (see Ministry of Justice, 2013, 2014; Prison Reform Trust, 2016).
- Sometimes, the adverse effects of socio-economic conditions of existence on behaviour have been acknowledged but cohabit with the expansion of the criminal justice domain. The neoliberal avalanche (Wacquant, 2008, 2009a) has rolled down the slope to inflict damage at the bottom of the class structure, and governments have responded with a dose of punishment and prison (see discussion in Chapter Two) rather than structural improvements.
- Restorative justice is an important sentencing aim (see Section 142 of the Criminal Justice Act 2003), but it is incompatible with retributive and deterrent punishment, which has displaced rehabilitation.
- The history, culture and social work tradition of probation has been subjected to repeated governmental assaults, which have convulsed the organisation. Its historic role in the system of criminal and social justice has been eroded through the creation of 21 community rehabilitation companies (CRCs) (for some interesting observations, see National Audit Office, 2014, 2016). This has badly damaged both criminal and social justice.

This is a history of inconsistency and contradiction, and heavy-handed and excessive intervention into criminal justice and penal policy. If Aristotle invites us to plough a path between *excess* and *deficiency* –

the Aristotelian *mean* – the recent history of criminal justice and penal policy operates at the extremity of punitive excess and moral deficiency (Whitehead, 2016a). Furthermore, from 1997 to 2010, through to 2015 and beyond, criminal justice has been seized by the technical requirements of numerical outcomes and measureable targets; a punishment, prisons and bureaucratic rationality to manage more than understand offending behaviours. These distinctive contours constitute the organisational logics of the new public management, in turn, supported and sustained by the ideological-material platform of the neoliberal capitalist order. This order has imposed a paradigm shift, indexed graphically by the traumatic disturbances experienced by the privatisation of most probation services.

When I refer to the ideological and material platform of neoliberal capitalism, I am reflecting on the release of competition, privatisation and marketised energies that care little for criminal and social justice, indifferent as they are to morality and reform. The system has been reduced to an instrumental function in order to achieve fiscal efficiencies and provide investment opportunities to the commercial sector, and 'payment by results' (Whitehead, 2015b) is the material signifier of this reconfiguration. Formerly, we operated within the framework of *penal-welfare* that exhorted a rehabilitative ethic; now, we are harried on all sides by punishment and incarceration. Reformism can only tinker at the edges, impose piecemeal adjustments and try to salvage something left behind by the modernisers, picking up any morsels of comfort that we can find. This is not a propitious context for reform. Conferences are attended each year to discuss reform precisely because there is much to reform. However, reformism has yielded few positive results during my nearly 40 years' involvement. In fact, the ethics of criminal justice has declined rather than advanced (see Eriksson, 2016). Criminal justice and penal policy have suffered many reverses from the lofty civilisational ideal of rehabilitation. It is logical to consider a different, a more fundamental, starting point for our discussions.

The criminal justice system cannot be *reformed* any more than capitalism can be reformed. Rather, it should be *transformed* by an ethically informed political act through a new ideological commitment. Here, ideology is not a distortion of, or escape from, reality, but *is* reality (Žižek, 1989). Ideology is the means by which to reorder the world beyond the neoliberal capitalist order of things by an alternative set of values and beliefs. Ideology is a transformative act to bring about a new political, ethical and organisational settlement. The criminal justice system of the social-democratic age has been overwritten by the ideological and material priorities of the neoliberal age. We, in turn, must overwrite the last 30 years. Future Howard League conferences should consider *reshaping the penal landscape through politico-economic transformation* rather than colluding with the pretence of reformism. We can no more entertain creating a Big Society (as aspirationally noble as this is), reforming criminal justice and penal policy, or reducing the pejorative other unless and until we address the politico-economic foundations of the neoliberal operating system. Unless we achieve this outcome, the system will continue to create the demonised and relegated other, which affects us all.

Notes

[1] Asbridge (2010) comments that the English and French assimilated the distant memory of crusades to assist their imperial heritage in the 19th century. Later, in the 20th and 21st centuries, we have witnessed, in some sections of the Muslim world, a tendency to 'equate modern political and religious struggles with holy wars witnessed nine centuries earlier' (Asbridge, 2010, p 2). Crusades exemplified recourse to violence in the name of God; fighting and dying in the name of God would gain entry to paradise. These events cast a long and dark shadow over West–East relations for centuries and continue to punch into the present era. It was a Roman Pope, Urban II, who launched the first crusade in 1095 to take up arms in the Latin West and fight in the name of Christianity – West and East, Latin and Greek, Christian and Muslim. Perversely, crusading was a form of devotion and for the medieval mind, there was little concern over the juxtaposition of religion and violence. When George W. Bush after 9/11 foolishly described his war on terror as a crusade, he played into the hands of Al Qaeda (Asbridge, 2010, p 679).

[2] The *Critique of pure reason* advances the thesis that human knowledge of the world is made possible because the subject, the transcendental ego or

self, determines the structure of our everyday experience. The mind and its innate ideas and categories of thought organises and transposes sense experience into an intelligible order by the forms of space and time as the *a priori* categories of understanding.

Concluding comment

We have a problem, a long-standing problem, aggravated and compounded by the weight of history. Its origins can be traced to the Agricultural Revolution when Homo sapiens started to live alongside each other in larger groups. Agricultural developments precipitated social problems, exposed by biological deficiencies (Harari, 2014), which were not adequately compensated for by religious myths or ethico-cultural scripts. Nevertheless, recorded history is not solely one of conflict. During the Axial Age (Jaspers, 1953), the Silk Roads linking East and West traded material goods but also ideas of peace, tolerance, even love. These ideas clashed with repeated bouts of violence and war, a 'contradiction that has plagued the whole of human history' (Scott, 2016, p 342). The accumulated weight of this contradiction reaches into the present to affect our relations with others.

The *problem* is conveyed in a collection of words that thread their way throughout this monograph: wasted lives, outsiders, scapegoats, urban outcasts, revolting subjects, the wretched of the earth, chavs, the demonised and the relegated other. The problem is *explained* by biological endowment, socialisation, politico-economic structures, ideology and religious, racial and ethnic fault lines (see also Smith, 2016). *Manifestations* of the demonised other include Nazi tyranny, refugee crises, the European problem (see Žižek, 2016; Murray, 2017) and the modernised criminal justice system that exacerbates pejorative othering through the excessive use of punishment and prison. *Responses* to the problem can be found in religious myths, imaginative scripts, ethics and culture, theology (Küng, 1977), sociology, psychoanalysis on the Symbolic order or Big Other, and moral economy. Significantly, transcendental materialism suggests that it is possible to change hearts and minds through creating a new Symbolic order or socio-symbolic system that would reduce othering. This will take time, being a long process and not one-off event, through immersion in an ideology that can reset our cognitive and emotional dealings with each other.

The daunting task before us is to construct the conditions of existence for our collective well-being and security as a species. Chapter Three assimilates some of the resources that we will need to stimulate the achievement of this task. So, what is our judgement? More of the same, repeating and reproducing the past, or seizing the moment to assert that we belong to one universal humanity, involving our interconnectedness, reverence for life, equality and sharing the earth's resources more justly and fairly – not self-aggrandisement at the expense of others, but a step towards each other in an act of mutual recognition. There are many obstacles in our path but fresh thinking is required to redirect the stream of history and its troubling legacies. This is the domain of ethics and politics, or how to organise ourselves in the best interests of all. To repeat, it is not possible to establish the Big Society or *a society that works for all*, resolve criminality, harm, punishment and prison in the modernised criminal justice system, or redirect the stream of history that frames this enquiry unless and until we confront the immediacies of neoliberal capitalism. This is a good place to start because of the subjectivity[1] it fashions, the desires and drives it elicits along with its relentless demands, and the many casualties of othering it produces. Neoliberal capitalism releases its psychotic energies to promote short-term gains for the few and lack of concern for the many – big bonus for me and austerity for you (Chomsky, 2016). Whoever we are and whatever our historical background, the blessings and burdens of accident of birth, religious affiliation and none, race and ethnic group, it is vital and urgent to rally around a flag that signals a universal commitment to respect for persons, reverence for life and our duties and obligations towards each other. Moral economy accommodates these universally binding features. These are the elements in a network of human relations that will give us a chance to enhance life on earth. We are confronted with a stark choice: life or death, light or dark, good or evil, the other as neighbour or as enemy.

From ancient empires to the neoliberal capitalist project, the world has been carved up into them and us, patrician and plebeian, free and slave, men and women, haves and have-nots, rich and poor. However, it is as vital and urgent now as at any time in the past to fashion an alternative politico-ethical order in which there is neither Jew nor Greek, Greek nor barbarian, free nor slave, wealthy nor poor, ruler nor ruled, Arab nor Israeli, Indian nor Pakistani, Turk nor Greek, Christian nor Muslim, and Protestant nor Catholic. If our ancestors created the conditions of existence for pejorative othering, it is up to us to repair the damage. To repeat the bold assertion at the beginning of this enquiry, the ethical question confronting all of us without exception, and with a pressing urgency, is how to live alongside each other where the other person is our neighbour, not our disposable or competitive enemy. If the conditions of existence under which we conduct our lives at any given moment is a contingent creation, if not a freakish biological accident (Dawkins, 2006; Harari, 2014), then the political and economic, the ethical and cultural, can be reconstructed to achieve different outcomes. The world that we have made over recent centuries can and must be remade. This will require dedicated political *and* ethical leadership that prioritises a vision of the good life for all, over one rigged to benefit the interests of the few: not Brexit, but one European and world community; not erecting walls of division between nations, but building bridges; and not aggressive competition, but cooperation between the peoples of the earth. To move in this direction will reduce demonising the other.

Note

[1] According to Badiou (cited in Žižek, 2016, p 84), there are three types of subjectivity: the Western middle-class liberal-democratic subject that reflects and reproduces the hegemonic order; those outside the Western zone of interest who desire to be like us; and fascist nihilists, death-cult

devotees, whose visceral envy of the West turns to hatred and violence with such catastrophic effects.

References

Ackroyd, P. (1983) *The last testament of Oscar Wilde*, London: Penguin.

Ackroyd, P. (2011) *The history of England volume 1: Foundation*, Basingstoke: Macmillan.

Amis, M. (2000) *Experience: A memoir*, New York, NY: Hyperion.

Amis, M. (2015) *The zone of interest*, London: Vintage.

Anderson, B.W. (1988) *The living world of the Old Testament*, Harlow: Longman.

Asbridge, T. (2010) *The Crusades: The war for the Holy Land*, London and New York, NY: Simon and Schuster.

Asim, J. (2007) *The N word, who can say it, who shouldn't, and why*, New York, NY: Mariner Books.

Barker, V. (2016) 'On Bauman's moral duty: population registries, REVA and eviction from the Nordic realm', in A. Eriksson (ed) *Punishing the Other: The social production of immorality*, Abingdon: Routledge.

Batchelor, J. (2000) *John Ruskin: No wealth but life*, London: Chatto and Windus.

Bauman, Z. (1989) *Modernity and the Holocaust*, Ithaca, NY: Cornell University Press.

Bauman, Z. (2000) *Liquid modernity*, Cambridge: Polity.

Bauman, Z. (2001) *The individualized society*, Cambridge: Polity.

Bauman, Z. (2004) *Wasted lives: Modernity and its outcasts*, Cambridge: Polity.

Beard, M. (2015) *SPQR: A history of ancient Rome*, London: Profile Books.

Becker, H. (1963) *Outsiders: Studies in the sociology of deviance*, London and New York, NY: The Free Press.

Bell, E. (2011) *Criminal justice and neoliberalism*, Houndmills: Palgrave Macmillan.

Berdyaev, N. (1935) *The fate of Man in the modern world*, London: SCM.

Bethge, E. (1970) *Dietrich Bonhoeffer: A biography*, London: Collins.

Beynon, H., Hudson, R. and Sadler, D. (1994) *A place called Teesside: A locality in a global economy*, Edinburgh: Edinburgh University Press.

Blackham, H.J. (1965) *Six existentialist thinkers*, Abingdon: Routledge and Kegan Paul.

Blumenfeld, B. (2001) *The political Paul: Justice, democracy and kingship in a Hellenistic framework*, London and New York, NY: Sheffield Academic Press.

Bonhoeffer, D. (1955) *Ethics*, London and New York, NY: Macmillan.

Bonhoeffer, D. (1963) *The communion of Saints*, London: Harper Row.

Bonhoeffer, D. (1966) *Christology*, London: Harper Row.

Bonhoeffer, D. (1971) *Letters and papers from prison* (ed E. Bethge), London: SCM.

Bonhoeffer, D. (1973) *True patriotism: Letters, lectures and notes 1939–45 from the collected works of Dietrich Bonhoeffer*, London: Collins.

Boulton, A. and Jones, J. (2010) *Hung together: The 2010 election and the Coalition Government*, London and New York, NY: Simon and Schuster.

Bruhn, A., Nylander, P.-A. and Lindberg, O. (2016) 'Swedish "prison exceptionalism" in decline: trends towards distantiation and objectification of the Other', in A. Eriksson (ed) *Punishing the Other: The social production of immorality*, Abingdon: Routledge.

Buber, M. (1970) *I and thou*, Edinburgh: T. and T. Clark.

Cabinet Office (2010a) *Transcript of David Cameron speech on the Big Society in Liverpool on 19 July 2010*, London: Cabinet Office.

Cabinet Office (2010b) *Modernising commissioning: Increasing the role of charities, social enterprises, mutuals and cooperatives in public service delivery*, Green Paper, London: Cabinet Office.

Cameron, D. (2013) 'The Prime Minister's Christmas message'. Available at: http://www.bbc.co.uk/news/uk-politics-25501333 (accessed 24 December 2013).

Carey, J. (2014) *The unexpected professor: An Oxford life in books*, London: Faber and Faber.

Carter, P. (2007) *Securing the future: Proposals for the efficient and sustainable use of custody in England and Wales*, London: Ministry of Justice.

Cavadino, M. and Dignan, J. (2006) *The penal system: An introduction*, London: Sage.

Chakraborti, N. and Garland, J. (2015) *Hate crime: Impact, causes and responses* (2nd edn), London: Sage.

Chomsky, N. (2016) *Who rules the world?*, London: Hamish Hamilton.

Civil Exchange (2013) *The Big Society audit*, London: Civil Exchange.

Cohen, S. (1973) *Folk devils and moral panics: The creation of the mods and rockers*, St. Albans: Paladin.

Conservative Party (2008) *A stronger society: Voluntary action for the 21st century*, London: Conservative Party.

Conservative Party (2010) *Invitation to join the government of Britain* (Conservative Party manifesto), London: Conservative Party.

Cook, D. (2006) *Criminal and social justice*, London, Thousand Oaks, CA, and New Delhi: Sage.

Copleston, F. (2003 [1946]) *Greece and Rome* (vol 1), London and New York, NY: Continuum.

Copleston, F. (2003 [1958]) *The rationalists: Descartes to Leibniz* (vol 4), London and New York, NY: Continuum.

Copleston, F. (2003 [1960]) *The Enlightenment: Voltaire to Kant* (vol 6), London and New York, NY: Continuum.

Copleston, F. (2003 [1975]) *19th and 20th century French philosophy* (vol 9), London and New York, NY: Continuum.

Coyle, A., Fair, H., Jacobson, J. and Walmsley, R. (2016) *Imprisonment worldwide: The current situation and an alternative future*, Bristol: The Policy Press.

Dawkins, R. (2006) *The God delusion*, London: Bantam Press.

De Giorgi, A. (2006) *Rethinking the political economy of punishment: Perspectives on post-Fordism and penal politics*, Aldershot: Ashgate.

Douzinas, C. (2013) *Philosophy and resistance in the crisis: Greece and the future of Europe*, Cambridge: Polity.

Dumas, A. (1971) *Dietrich Bonhoeffer: Theologian of reality*, London: SCM.

Eagleton, T. (2009) *Trouble with strangers: A study of ethics*, Chichester: Wiley-Blackwell.

Elias, N. (1994) *The civilising process: Sociogenetic and psychogenetic investigations*, Oxford: Blackwell.

Elliott, A. (2005) 'Psychoanalytic social theory', in A Harrington (ed) *Modern social theory: An introduction*, Oxford and New York, NY: Oxford University Press.

Erikson, K.T. (1966) *Wayward puritans: A study in the sociology of deviance*, Chichester: Wiley.

Eriksson, A. (ed) (2016) *Punishing the Other: The social production of immorality*, Abingdon: Routledge.

Faulks, S. (2015) *Where my heart used to beat*, London: Hutchinson.

Foucault, M. (1977) *Discipline and punish: The birth of the prison*, Peregrine Books.

Frankopan, P. (2015) *The Silk Roads: A new history of the world*, London: Bloomsbury.

Garland, D. (1985) *Punishment and welfare: A history of penal strategies*, Aldershot: Gower.

Garland, D. (1990) *Punishment and modern society: A study in social theory*, Oxford and New York, NY: Oxford University Press.

Garland, D. (2001) *The culture of control: Crime and social disorder in contemporary society*, Oxford and New York, NY: Oxford University Press.

Giddens, A. (1971) *Capitalism and modern social theory: An analysis of the writings of Marx, Durkheim and Max Weber*, Cambridge: Cambridge University Press.

Gill, A. (1988) *The journey back from hell: An oral history. Conversations with concentration camp survivors*, William Morrow and Company.

Gill, A.A. (2015) 'Migrant crisis special: the long, painful road to Europe', *Sunday Times Magazine*, 18 October.

Gosling, G. (2012) 'Charity and the Coalition: whatever happened to the Big Society?'. Available at: at: http://www.vahs.org.uk/2012/04/coalition-gosling/ (accessed 1 December 2013).

Götz, N. (2015) 'Moral economy: its conceptual history and analytical prospects', *Journal of Global Ethics*, 11(2): 147–62.

Hall, S. (2012) *Theorising crime and deviance: A new perspective*, London: Sage.

Hall, S. (2014) 'The socioeconomic function of evil', *The Sociological Review*, 62(S2): 13–31.

Hall, S. and Winlow, S. (2015) *Revitalizing criminological theory: Towards a new ultra realism*, London and New York, NY: Routledge.

Hall, S., Winlow, S. and Ancrum, C. (2008) *Criminal identities and consumer culture: Crime, exclusion and the new culture of narcissism*, Cullompton: Willan.

Hand, S. (ed) (1989) *The Levinas reader*, Oxford: Blackwell.

Harari, Y.N. (2014) *Sapiens: A brief history of humankind*, London: Harvill Secker.

Harrington, A. (ed) (2005) *Modern social theory: An introduction*, Oxford and New York, NY: Oxford University Press.

Harvey, D. (2005) *A brief history of neoliberalism*, Oxford and New York, NY: Oxford University Press.

Harvey, D. (2010) *The enigma of capital and the crises of capitalism*, London: Profile Books.

HM Government (2010a) *The Coalition: Our programme for government*, London: HM Government.

HM Government (2010b) *Building a stronger society: A strategy for voluntary and community groups, charities and social enterprises*, London: Office for Civil Society, Cabinet Office.

Holland, T. (2015) *Dynasty: The rise and fall of the House of Caesar*, London: Little Brown.

Home Office (1977) *A review of criminal justice policy 1976*, London: HMSO.

Homer, S. (2005) *Jacques Lacan*, London and New York, NY: Routledge.

Hudson, B. (1993) *Penal policy and social justice*, Houndmills: Macmillan.

Hume, D. (1983 [1777]) *An enquiry concerning the principles of morals* (ed J.B. Schneewind), Indianapolis, IN, and Cambridge: Hackett Publishing Company.

Ishkanian, A. and Szreter, S. (eds) (2012) *The Big Society debate: A new agenda for social welfare*, Cheltenham: Edward Elgar Publishing.

Jameson, F. (1991) *Postmodernism, or, the cultural logic of late capitalism*, London: Verso.

Jaspers, K. (1953) *The origin and goal of history*, London: Routledge & Kegan Paul.

Jones, E. (1968) *Profiles of the prophets*, Oxford: The Religious Education Press.

Jones, O. (2015) *The establishment: And how they get away with it*, Harmondsworth: Penguin.

Jordan, B. (2010) *Why the Third Way failed: Economics, morality and the origins of the 'Big Society'*, Bristol: The Policy Press.

Juncker, J.-C. (2015) *Completing Europe's economic and monetary union: The five president's report*, European Commission.

Jütte, R. (1994) *Poverty and deviance in early modern Europe*, Cambridge: Cambridge University Press.

Kant, I. (2005 [1785]) *The moral law: Groundwork of the metaphysics of morals*, Abingdon: Routledge.

Katz, M.B. (1989) *The undeserving poor: From the war on poverty to the war on welfare*, New York, NY: Pantheon Books.

Kershaw, I. (2015) *To hell and back: Europe 1914–1949*, London: Allen Lane.

Kiberd, D. (2009) *Ulysses and us: The art of everyday living*, London: Faber and Faber.

Kotzé, J. (2016) 'Analysing the "crime decline": change and continuity in crime and harm', unpublished PhD thesis, School of Social Sciences, Business and Law, Teesside University.

Küng, H. (1977) *On being a Christian*, London: Collins.

Lacan, J. (2001) *Écrits*, Abingdon: Routledge.

Levi, P. (1987) *If this is a man and the truce*, London: Abacus.

Leys, C. (2003) *Market-driven politics: Neoliberal democracy and the public interest*, London and New York, NY: Verso.

Lindsey, R. and Bulloch, S.L. (2013) *What the public think of the 'Big Society': Mass observers' views on individual and community capacity for civic engagement*, Working Paper 95, London: Third Sector Research Centre.

MacIntyre, A. (1967) *A short history of ethics*, London: Routledge and Kegan Paul.

Maskell, R. (2010) 'UNITE criticises the Big Society as intellectually flawed'. Available at: http://www.charitytimes.com/ct/Big_Society_Unite.plp (accessed 1 March 2013).

Mead, R. (2014) *The road to Middlemarch: My life with George Eliot*, London: Granta.

Metaxas, E. (2010) *Bonhoeffer pastor, martyr, prophet, spy: A righteous gentile vs. the Third Reich*, Nashville, TN: Thomas Nelson.

Metzger, B.M. and Coogan, M.D. (1993) *The Oxford companion to the Bible*, Oxford and New York, NY: Oxford University Press.

Ministry of Justice (2013) *Story of the prison population: 1993–2012 England and Wales*, January, London: Ministry of Justice.

Ministry of Justice (2014) *Prison population projections 2014–2020 England and Wales*, Statistical Bulletin, November, London: Ministry of Justice.

Mirowski, P. (2013) *Never let a serious crisis go to waste: How neoliberalism survived the financial meltdown*, London: Verso.

Mounier, E. (1952) *Personalism*, Notre Dame: University of Notre Dame Press.

Mozley, E.N. (1950) *The theology of Albert Schweitzer for Christian enquirers*, London: Adam and Charles Black.

Murray, C. (1984) *Losing ground*, New York, NY: Basic Books.

Murray, C. (1990) *The emerging underclass*, London: Institute of Economic Affairs.

Murray, C. (1994) *Underclass: The crisis deepens*, London: Institute of Economic Affairs.

Murray, D. (2017) *The strange death of Europe: Immigration, identity, Islam*, London and New York, NY: Bloomsbury.

Myers, T. (2003) *Slavoj Žižek*, Abingdon: Routledge.

National Audit Office (2014) *Probation: Landscape review*, London: National Audit Office.

National Audit Office (2016) *Transforming probation*, London: National Audit Office.

National Council for Voluntary Organisations (2010) *Briefing on the 'Big Society'*, London: NCVO Policy Team.

New Economics Foundation (2010) *Cutting it: The 'Big Society' and the new austerity*, London: New Economics Foundation.

Nicholson, A. (2014) *The mighty dead: Why Homer matters*, London: William Collins.

Norman, J. (2010) *The Big Society: The anatomy of the new politics*, Buckingham: The University of Buckingham Press.

Olson, R.G. (1962) *An introduction to existentialism*, New York, NY: Dover Publications.

Orwell, G. (1933) *Down and out in Paris and London*, London: Penguin.

Peters, J. (2012) 'Neoliberal convergence in North America and Western Europe: fiscal austerity, privatization, and public sector reform', *Review of International Political Economy*, 19(2): 208–35.

Plato (1974) *Republic*, Harmondsworth: Penguin.

Postan, M.M. (1972) *The Medieval economy and society: An economic history of Britain 1100–1500*, London: Weidenfeld and Nicholson.

Prison Reform Trust (2016) *Prison: The facts, Bromley briefing summer 2016*, London: Prison Reform Trust.

Reiner, R. (2007) *Law and order: An honest citizen's guide to crime and control*, Cambridge: Polity.

Rhodes, D. (2011) *Capitalism, sustainability and the Big Society: Meeting the global challenge of ensuring a sustainable future*, Milton Keynes: AuthorHouse.

Riello, G. (2013) *Cotton: The fabric that made the modern world*, Cambridge: Cambridge University Press.

Rodger, J.J. (2008) *Criminalising social policy: Anti-social behaviour and welfare in a de-civilised society*, Cullompton: Willan.

Rodger, J.J. (2013) '"New capitalism", colonisation and the neo-philanthropic turn in social policy: applying Luhmann's systems theory to the Big Society project', *International Journal of Sociology and Social Policy*, 33(11/12): 725–41.

Rule, J. (1995) *The vital century: England's developing economy 1714–1815*, London and New York, NY: Longman.

Rusche, G. and Kirchheimer, O. (1968 [1939]) *Punishment and social structure*, New York, NY: Russell and Russell.

Russell, B. (1946) *History of Western philosophy*, London and New York, NY: Routledge.

Russell, L.M. (1941) *The path to reconstruction: A brief introduction to Albert Schweitzer's philosophy of civilization*, London: Adam and Charles Black.

Sainsbury, E. (1977) *Personal social services*, London: Pitman.

Sandel, M. (2012) *What money can't buy: The moral limits of markets*, London and New York, NY: Allen Lane.

Sands, P. (2016) *East West Street: On the origins of genocide and crimes against humanity*, London: Weidenfeld & Nicholson.

Sartre, J.-P. (1948) *Existentialism and humanism*, London: Eyre Methuen Ltd.

Schweitzer, A. (1929) *Civilisation and ethics: The philosophy of civilisation, part 2* (2nd edn), London: A. and C. Black.

Schweitzer, A. (1955) *On the edge of the primeval forest*, London: A. and C. Black.

Schweitzer, A. (1961) *The decay and restoration of civilisation: The philosophy of civilisation, part 1*, London: Unwin.

Schweitzer, A. (1962) *My childhood and youth*, London: Unwin.

Scott, M. (2016) *Ancient worlds: An epic history of East and West*, London: Windmill Books.

Seaver, G. (1947) *Albert Schweitzer: The man and his mind*, London: A. and C. Black.

Shipman, T. (2016) *All out war: The full story of how Brexit sank Britain's political class*, London: William Collins.

Sim, J. (2009) *Punishment and prisons: Power and the carceral state*, London: Thousand Oaks, CA and New Delhi: Sage.

Simon, J. (2016) 'The legal civilizing process: dignity and the protection of human rights in advanced bureaucratic democracies', in A. Eriksson (ed) *Punishing the Other: The social production of immorality*, Abingdon: Routledge.

Singer, P. (1983) *Hegel: A very short introduction*, Oxford and New York, NY: Oxford University Press.

Smith, A. (2009 [1759]) *The theory of moral sentiments* (intro by A. Sen), London and New York, NY: Penguin.

Smith, P.S. (2016) 'Dehumanization, social contact and techniques of Othering: combining the lessons from Holocaust studies and prison research', in A. Eriksson (ed) *Punishing the Other: The social production of immorality*, Abingdon: Routledge.

Solomon, R.C. (1988) *Continental philosophy since 1750: The rise and fall of the self*, Oxford and New York, NY: Oxford University Press.

Standing, G. (2011) *The precariat: The new dangerous class*, London: Bloomsbury.

Stedman-Jones, G. (1971) *Outcast London: A study in the relationship between the classes in Victorian society*, Oxford: Clarendon Press.

Steiner, R. (1973) *The riddles of philosophy*, Steiner Books.

Stevenson, L. and Haberman, D.L. (1998) *Ten theories of human nature*, Oxford and New York, NY: Oxford University Press.

Stuckler, D. and Basu, S. (2013) *The body economic: Why austerity kills*, London: Allen Lane.

Taubes, J. (2004) *The political theology of Paul*, Stanford, CA: Stanford University Press.

Temple, D. (2016) 'News from nowhere: reconceptualising desistance', unpublished PhD thesis, School of Social Sciences, Business and Law, Teesside University, UK.

Theroux, P. (2015) *Deep South: Four seasons on the back roads*, London: Hamish Hamilton.

Thomas, H. (1998) *The slave trade: The history of the Atlantic slave trade 1440–1870*, London: Papermac.

Thompson, E.P. (1971) 'The moral economy of the English crowd in the eighteenth century', *Past and Present*, 50: 76–136.

Tyler, I. (2013) *Revolting subjects: Social abjection and resistance in neoliberal Britain*, London and New York, NY: Zed Books.

United Nations Office on Drugs and Crime (2016) *Global report on trafficking in persons*, New York, NY: UNODC.

Wachsmann, N. (2015) *A history of the Nazi concentration camps*, New York, NY: Little Brown.

Wacquant, L. (2001) 'Deadly symbiosis: when ghetto and prison meet and mesh', *Punishment & Society*, 3(1): 95–133.

Wacquant, L. (2008) *Urban outcasts: A comparative sociology of advanced marginality*, Cambridge: Polity.

Wacquant, L. (2009a) *Punishing the poor: The neoliberal government of social insecurity*, Durham and London: Duke University Press.

Wacquant, L. (2009b) *Prisons of poverty*, Minneapolis, MN: University of Minnesota Press.

Ward-Perkins, B. (2005) *The fall of Rome and the end of civilisation*, Oxford: Oxford University Press.

Whitehead, P. (2015a) *Reconceptualising the moral economy of criminal justice: A new perspective*, Houndmills: Palgrave.

Whitehead, P. (2015b) 'Payment by results: the materialist reconstruction of criminal justice', *International Journal of Sociology and Social Policy*, 35(5/6): 290–305.

Whitehead, P. (2016a) *Transforming probation: Social theories and the criminal justice system*, Bristol: The Policy Press.

Whitehead, P. (2016b) '"Shine like a jewel": Kantian ethics, probation duty and criminal justice', *European Journal of Probation*, 8(2): 51–67.

Whitehead, P. and Crawshaw, P. (2014) 'A tale of two economies: the political and the moral in neoliberalism', *International Journal of Sociology and Social Policy*, 34(1/2): 19–34.

Whitehead, P. and Hall, S. (forthcoming) 'The generative core overpowered the regulatory sleeve: the fate of public institutions from the Keynesian settlement to the neoliberal order'.

Wilde, O. (1986) *De profundis and other writings*, London: Penguin Classics.

Wilkinson, R. and Pickett, K. (2009) *The spirit level: Why more equal societies almost always do better*, London and New York, NY: Allen Lane.

Williams, R. (2012) *Faith in the public square*, London and New York, NY: Bloomsbury.

Winlow, S. and Hall, S. (2013) *Rethinking social exclusion: The end of the social?*, London: Sage.

Winlow, S., Hall, S., Treadwell, J. and Briggs, D. (2015) *Riots and political protest: Notes from the post-political present*, London and New York, NY: Routledge.

Winlow, S., Hall, S. and Treadwell, J. (2016) *The rise of the Right: English nationalism and the transformation of working-class politics*, Bristol: The Policy Press.

Wright, N.T. (2009) *Justification: God's plan and Paul's vision*, London: SPCK.

Young, J. (2007) *The vertigo of late modernity*, London: Sage.

Žižek, S. (1989) *The sublime object of ideology*, London: Verso.

Žižek, S. (1992) *Looking awry: An introduction to Jacques Lacan through popular culture*, Cambridge, MA, and London: The MIT Press.

Žižek, S. (2006) *How to read Lacan*, London: Granta Books.

Žižek, S. (2010) 'A meditation on Michelangelo's *Christ on the cross*', in J. Milbank, S. Žižek and C. Davis (eds) *Paul's new moment: Continental philosophy and the future of Christian theology*, Michigan, MI: Brazos Press.

Žižek, S. (2014) *Event*, London: Penguin.

Žižek, S. (2016) *Against the double blackmail: Refugees, terror and other troubles with the neighbours*, London: Allen Lane.

Index

Note: Page numbers followed by an "n" indicate end-of-chapter notes